Handling Small Boats in Heavy Weather

By the same author:
Sea Hunters Longmans, 1950
Fisherman of the Cape (with Bruce Franck) Longmans, 1975

Frank Robb

Handling
Small Boats
in Heavy Weather

Quadrangle/The New York Times Book Co.

First published in Great Britain
by Adlard Coles Limited.

Library of Congress Catalog Card Number: 76-168607
SBN 8129-0217-3

PRINTED IN GREAT BRITAIN

DEDICATION
To Connie Bond—for faith

Contents

Illustrations

The photographs of Force 9 and 10 seas on pages 18, 32, 35, 45, 48, 52, 65, 76, 80, 96 and 121 are all by Captain D A de Lange

Master of this ship under God

'—the Captain's mantle—that almost visible aura of responsibility that surrounds the Master of any boat, irrespective of his character or nature. It is an inescapable burden, a price to be paid without haggling or bargaining. The sea takes no heed of truth or falsehood; honesty and chicanery are as one to it, and no exercise of these qualities will distract it or deflect its blows. A Captain, be he saint or sinner, must pay the inexorable fee in the only currencies that the sea honours—duty, vigilance, skill and endurance.'

'No Skipper, be his boat large or small, notes with pleasure a falling barometer, a brassy sunset, a big swell and the prospect of what may follow. Engines can fail, rudders carry away, freak seas smash down—things to be neither foreseen nor forestalled. Might not this same gale now portending be the legendary Masterwind—the Wrath of God that would some day rage to rip plank from timber, breath from body, and lash the very oceans from their beds to drown all the lands?'

Sea Hunters

Foreword

This is not another 'How to Sail' book.

It is written for the owners and/or skippers of small sea-going boats—motor or sail, commercial or pleasure—who are satisfied that they can handle their boats competently in 'normal' weather—i.e. up to gale force.

This is a book about abnormal weather. Any sea-goer must face the fact that he may be caught-out in hurricane winds and seas against which his 'normal' defences will not prevail. He must adopt different tactics, and this book deals with these tactics.

It is, in fact, not a 'Sailing' book at all, for it is concerned mainly with hurricane conditions in which no boat could carry any sail. It might justly be entitled 'Survival at Sea'. It is a distillation of forty-five years of skippering small sailing and motor vessels. The venues include the Mediterranean and the United Kingdom, but mostly the sea-board of Southern Africa—off the Cape of Storms which claims the doubtful distinction of being second only to Cape Horn for savage weather.

When writing for the initiated one expects criticism—informed or otherwise. There is much in this book that will arouse howls of protest not only from the 'Armchair Vikings' but also from some experienced cruising men, to whom some of the recommendations may appear to be a mere clinging to tradition, or a mulish refusal to accept new ideas and theories in deep-sea thinking.

But—let critics bear in mind that this book is written specifically for men and about boats cruising in latitudes in which they may become involved in catastrophic hurricane conditions.

Cape Town   Frank Robb

I

Weather

As Mark Twain said, 'People are always grumbling about the weather—but nobody ever *does* anything about it'.

One day Mankind may be able to control the weather, but that day has not yet dawned. In the meantime we have to take it as it comes. We have, however, learned a good deal about the causes of 'weather', and with the aid of a few simple instruments and a bit of horse-sense we can make an educated guess as to what the future holds in store. This is a useful bit of information—particularly for the small-boat Skipper. And so—for a start—let's discuss what makes the weather tick.

The Sun is the main-spring. It powers (directly or indirectly) all the winds that blow. Figure 1 gives an idealised picture of the Earth as a smooth sphere evenly heated around Equatorial regions. The hot air rises and the more dense cold air from Polar regions flows in to replace it. The figure shows that with such a system all winds would be either due North or due South.

But the Earth is not a smooth stationary ball. It rotates every 24 hours—which means that every point on its surface is moving Eastward at a speed which is minimum (nil) at the Poles and maximum (1,000 mph) at the Equator. The cold winds starting from the polar regions know nothing about this rotation (it took men a few thousands of years to discover it): they continue to blow due 'South' or due 'North'—and the Earth 'rolls away' underneath them. This is known as the

15

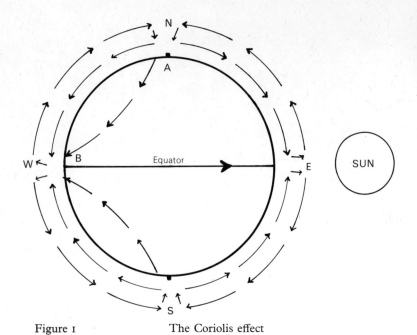

Figure 1   The Coriolis effect

Coriolis effect. Figure 1 shows how a cold wind starting at A at the North Pole and blowing due South will have its apparent direction increasingly deflected towards the West by the Earth rolling away underneath it, until in Equatorial regions it is blowing almost due West. This is a basic and important effect; in real life it is complicated by side effects (see below)—but it accounts for the South-East and the North-East Trade Winds, the Monsoon and the direction of rotation of Cyclonic systems (see Chapter 4). Winds blowing from the South Polar regions acquire a Westerly component for the same reason.

An additional effect of this preponderance of Easterly winds in 'low' (Equatorial) Latitudes is the generation of a return circuit of Westerly belts of winds in the high Latitudes. (Figure 2.) Between the Equatorial Easterlies and the Polar Westerlies we get friction—variables, depressions and, generally, eddies of winds.

If the Earth were completely covered with water the winds would behave in a fairly predictable manner. Figure 2 shows

Figure 2

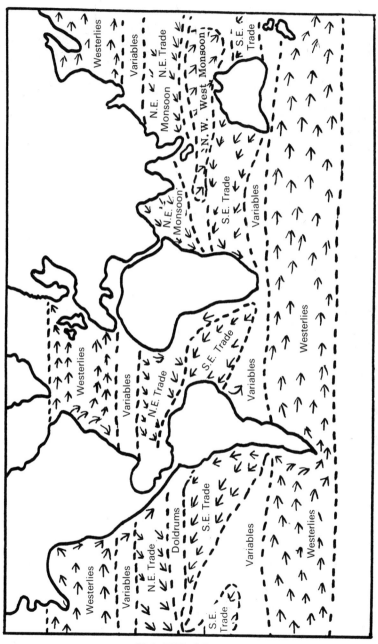

Global Wind System
(about February)

that over the larger areas of unbroken ocean it conforms to pattern, with the Easterly Trades blowing steadily throughout the year, the Westerly belts marching along in the higher Latitudes.

But the Earth is not a globe of water. There are large

chunks of land sticking up most untidily all over the place, and what this does to our orderly system of winds is one of the things that keeps the cruising man from boredom. Figure 2 shows how land masses obstruct and deflect the 'permanent' winds, causing them to lose their identity. The Atlantic Trades collide with the Americas. The Monsoon comes to grief on the shores of Africa, and there is so much land in the Northern Hemisphere that the Westerly Belt there is distorted almost out of recognition. Only the Roaring Forties down South find a clear path to keep blowing steadily throughout the year.

To make confusion worse the confounded land heats up during the day and cools off at night faster than the water does—which means that any large land mass generates its own local systems of winds. On top of it all the Sun wanders, bringing winter and summer to both Hemispheres—and causes further aberrations.

We have not completed the list of land's offences against orderliness. Surface water, urged along by the warm Trade Winds, literally piles up against the continental masses and finds outlets in the form of vast currents such as the Gulf Stream and the Mozambique Current—which in turn alter the temperature of the sea and the air above it thousands of miles from their sources and govern the climates of entire Continents.

In short, our orderly system of winds has become a sort of witch's cauldron capable of brewing up all sorts of un-expectednesses and surrounded on all sides by Weather Forecasters with stomach ulcers.

Many cruising men are not interested in the 'mechanism' of the weather, and rely on their radio for weather forecasts. But your radio man may be a long way from where you are (*and* in a different climate), and if you can keep the broad pattern of the wind and weather at the back of your mind it will help you a lot in filling in the gaps and drawing a picture of the weather trend in your own vicinity.

19

2

Instruments

Big boat man or small boat man, the sailor wants to know whence the wind will come, its strength, direction, probable change of strength and direction, sea and visibility conditions —and how long it is likely to last. To do this he should have the ability to supplement the radio forecasts, (which may refer to a different locality) by his own observations and to estimate the weather pattern in his own vicinity.

If, for instance, there is a gale in the offing he must try to find out as much as possible about probable future local conditions to enable him to make a decision as to whether he can dodge the gale by altering course, or whether he should (or must) sit tight and ride it out.

A good deal of assistance is nowadays available to him. Apart from the radio, he has the evidence of his own senses— never to be underestimated. If you get an uneasy feeling that dirty weather is on the way, don't ignore it: it is an instinct that all living creatures have, and it precedes the radio broadcasts by some millions of years. After a spell on the clean sea, with your mind and senses purged of the smog and superficialities of civilisation, you will find that this instinct is seldom wrong. Ask any sea-gull.

In addition you have the assistance of a number of more or less modern gadgets. Let us deal with these singly and simply.

Magnetic Compass. For noting the direction of winds,

alteration of direction—and which way to go to avoid trouble.

Radio. Listen to the weather-man. His guess is likely to be more educated than yours. Write it down—so that five minutes or so later you can check that he said North-West and not North-East. Even if you are in mid-ocean a report from a place hundreds of miles away can be of the utmost use in making your own local prediction. The radio forecast is, of course, not infallible. On more than one occasion I have been hanging on by the eyebrows in a full gale while listening to that cultured voice affirming that the wind was—light to moderate. Nevertheless and as stated above, the radio man has access to information which gives him a much broader picture—so listen to him.

Your radio should tune the Marine/Aviation band. Get a list of such stations and of the time of their weather forecasts. (Also note what language they use—it's so much easier if you can understand what the gentleman is saying.)

Alarm Clock. A must on every small boat. To remind you that it is time for the weather report—and useful for a dozen other occasions.

Barometer. A must. See Chapter 12. A mercury barometer is an unhandy thing in a small boat. An aneroid barometer is better, but a barograph is best. If you use the latter, suspend it in a cradle of springs or otherwise cushion it against shocks because if you don't it will make like a seismograph every time you bash into a head sea.

This is the basic instrument for weather forecasting.

Every region has its own barometric behaviour, and in the scope of this book it is not possible to go into local barometric peculiarities. Your Pilotage Manual tells you how to interpret the barometric pattern for any locality, but some general rules are worth remembering.

Most of these have come down to us in the form of little versicles of some antiquity—which is a good idea, because it makes them more memorable. I have taken the liberty of adding a couple of my own in more modern style.

At sea with a low and falling glass
The greenhorn sleeps like a careless ass
But when the glass is high and risin'
Soundly sleeps the careful wise 'un.

High and steady ?—Sleep at rest.
Sea will be flat as a typiste's chest.

Long foretold—long last.
Soon foretold—soon past.

Low and steady ? You can bet
Wind and sea are hand in glove.
The gale will last a good while yet.
Oh for the wings of a dove.

First rise after low fall
Brings the strongest blast of all.

None of the above rhymes are gospel, of course—but they indicate the general trend, and in mid-ocean are fairly reliable. Land in the vicinity can distort the picture. Where I was raised, for instance, two parallel mountain ranges form a venturi which on summer afternoons frequently produces a famous wind known as the Cape Doctor which pounces without warning, blowing from a cloudless sky and sometimes working up to 60 knots or more within minutes—and the barograph draws a dead straight line throughout the performance. All due to the presence of 'dat ole debbil' land. So remember that the barometer tends to indicate what the weather would be like in the absence of earthy excrescences upon the fair and lovely face of the sea.

Radio weather forecasts refer to barometric readings either

in millibars or in inches. The conversion is: 3.4 millibars =
0.1 inch. But it is easier to cut out the Inch/Millibar Conversion Table from last year's nautical almanac and paste it
up (with waterproof glue) near the barometer.

Thermometers. An air thermometer costs little and can be
useful. It has, however, no imagination, and if you hang it
in the cabin it will persist in indicating cabin temperature.

A water temperature thermometer is most useful. For one
thing, it will nearly always indicate whether you are just in
or out of a particular current.

Wet-and-dry bulb thermometers, hygrometers and anemometers are for savants. The latter indicates wind-force
and (for the cruising man) its only real use is to enable him
to boast about the strength of the gale he so cleverly survived.

3

Highs and Lows

The theory and practice of weather forecasting would fill a book larger than this, and if you would like to know more about this fascinating subject you will find a number of such books available. In this chapter we must be content with condensing enough of it to enable you to predict the main probable trends—which is as much as the cruising man hopes for.

Most of our weather, bad and good, comes to us in the form of large and roughly circular systems of winds circulating about a centre of high or low air pressure. (Figure 3.)

If the centre is low pressure the system is called cyclonic. Or, for short, a low, or a depression.

If the centre is high pressure the system is called anticyclonic. Or, for short, a high.

In the North Hemisphere the wind revolves anti-clockwise about a low, clockwise about a high.

In the South Hemisphere it revolves clockwise about a low, anti-clockwise about a high.

In both Hemispheres the wind spirals towards the direction of lower pressure. That is, inwards in a low, outwards in a high. The inclination of the wind towards the centre of a low is between 10° and 20°.

Characteristics of a high. Weather usually fine, winds light, but increasing towards the perimeter. The forward speed of the system as a whole is normally slow and sometimes it is

Figure 3 a,b,c,d

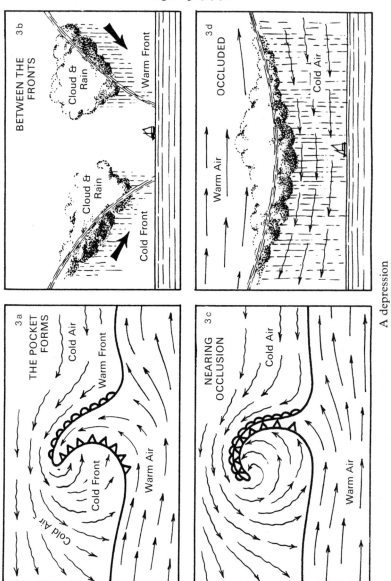

A depression

stationary. At points where it impinges on a different system the weather may be unsettled with cloud, wind and rain. A high tends to be a stable system.

Characteristics of a low. Weather deteriorates progressively from outskirts to centre. Speed of advance variable but generally faster than that of a high. The direction of advance is usually towards the area of lowest barometric pressure in the vicinity, and once established for twelve hours the direction usually alters slowly, if at all.

Formation of a depression. When two air streams of different characteristics meet, the line of demarcation between them is called a Front, (figure 3a) and along this front occur local inter-penetrations by one or other of the streams, with the warmer air forming a pocket into the colder air and at the same time rising over it and causing a area of low pressure at the bottom of the pocket. (Figure 3b.) Air flows towards this area and is deflected to the east by the rotation of the earth, thus becoming a system of winds rotating about a centre of low pressure—in other words, a low.

The cold air, being forced into a circle, encroaches upon the warm air, which rises over it, and the pocket is gradually narrowed. The line of this encroachment is called the cold front. (Figure 3b.) The opposite side of the pocket, where the warm air encroaches on the cold air and rises over it is called the warm front. In due course the cold front catches up with the warm front, all the warm air is lifted from the sea, and the system is said to be occluded. After which it dies out because the warm air was what provided the energy to maintain it. (Figure 3c and 3d.) The whole system moves along the line of the original front at a speed varying from about 10 to 70 knots.

That, then, is the birth and death of a depression, whence cometh most of our bad weather.

4

Hurricanes, Cyclones and Typhoons

Different names for the same thing—a tropical revolving storm. They originate in tropical zones, and are vast whirlwinds with a centre of low pressure; to that extent they resemble an ordinary Low and they obey the rotational law (anti-clockwise in the North Hemisphere, clockwise in the South Hemisphere).

They do not appear to be caused by neighbouring fronts of cold and warm air, but rather by some system of convection which is not fully understood. With the possible exception of water-spouts (tornadoes), they provide the strongest winds a sailor encounters, and their habits have been studied for many years, so that we have a pretty clear idea of the laws they obey.

Fortunately they are seasonal and choosey about their area of operation, so if you don't want to encounter one you simply steer clear of their stamping ground during the breeding season (see the **Seasons** list below). They are obviously something to be avoided if possible, and the following definitions, prognostications and rules will help you to steer clear of them.

The Hurricane, Typhoon and Cyclone Seasons

West Indies. June to November. Most frequent in September.

South Indian Ocean. October to June. Most frequent December to April.

China Sea. Throughout the year. Most frequent during October.

Arabian Sea. April to January. Most frequent June, October and November.

Bay of Bengal. May to December. Most frequent in September.

South Pacific. December to April. Most frequent January to March.

North Pacific. Throughout the year. Most frequent July to October.

Some definitions
(Figures 4a and 4b.)

Vortex, centre, or eye. An area of comparative calm in the centre of the storm. It is said to average about 8 miles in diameter, with winds light, variable or calm, but with a dangerous cross-sea.

The track. The direction in which the system is moving. This is at first westerly (see figure 4), curving towards the nearest Pole, and may later become north-east (N. Hemisphere) or south-east (S. Hemisphere). Not all cyclones follow this rule; some have erratic tracks, and in the Bay of Bengal they are said to have straight tracks.

Vertex or cod. The most westerly point reached by the centre before the cyclone recurves to the east.

Right semicircle. That half of the storm to the right of an observer looking along the track in the direction of travel.

Left semicircle. That half of the storm to the left of an observer looking along the track in the direction of travel.

Figure 4a and 4b

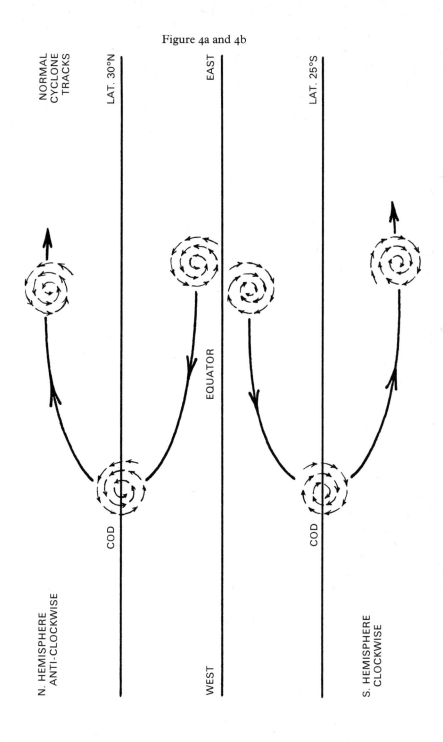

NORMAL CYCLONE TRACKS

LAT. 30°N

EAST

EQUATOR

WEST

LAT. 25°S

COD

COD

N. HEMISPHERE
ANTI-CLOCKWISE

S. HEMISPHERE
CLOCKWISE

Navigable semicircle. That half of the storm lying on the side of the track furthest from the direction in which it normally re-curves.

Trough. A line through the centre of the storm. at right-angles to the track.

Dangerous quadrant. That quadrant in which a ship would tend to be blown towards the path of the track. It is the advanced right-hand quadrant in the N. Hemisphere, the advanced left-hand quadrant in the S. Hemisphere.

Cyclones originate between Latitudes 10° and 20° on either side of the Equator. The total diameter of the storm may be over 1,000 miles, with a belt of hurricane-force winds between 5 and 65 miles wide spiralling in towards the eye in the centre.

The speed of advance is 6 to 8 knots at birth. This may later increase to as much as 50 knots.

The Cod is usually about 30°N. Latitude or 20°S. Latitude. (Figure 4.)

Signs and portents
1 *Unaccountable swell.* This moves out from the centre of the cyclone and its direction gives a good indication of the bearing of the centre. It may be felt at a distance of over 1,000 miles, and is usually likely to be felt at 400 miles. *If the storm is more than 200 miles away the direction of the swell is the most reliable indication of the bearing of the centre.*
2 Abnormal behaviour of the barometer.
3 High cirrus clouds, especially if in converging streaks or bands. The centre probably lies in the direction of the point of convergence.
4 Sultry, oppressive weather and a general uneasy feeling.

To find the bearing of the centre
Face the wind. The centre will be from 12 to 8 points

Figure 5

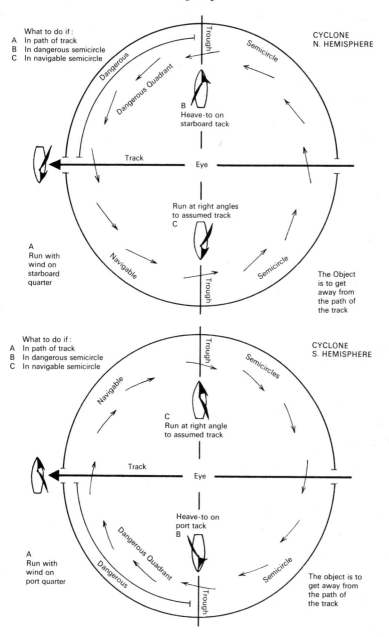

What to do if:
A In path of track
B In dangerous semicircle
C In navigable semicircle

CYCLONE
N. HEMISPHERE

Dangerous Semicircle

Trough

Dangerous Quadrant

B
Heave-to on
starboard tack

Semicircle

Track

Eye

Run at right angles
to assumed track
C

Navigable

Trough

Semicircle

A
Run with
wind on
starboard
quarter

The Object
is to get
away from
the path of
the track

What to do if:
A In path of track
B In dangerous semicircle
C In navigable semicircle

CYCLONE
S. HEMISPHERE

Trough

Semicircles

Navigable

C
Run at right angle
to assumed track

Track

Eye

Heave-to on
port tack
B

Dangerous Quadrant

Dangerous

Trough

Semicircle

A
Run with
wind on
port quarter

The object is to
get away from
the path of
the track

(135° to 90°) on the *right* hand in the Northern Hemisphere, on the *left* hand in the Southern Hemisphere.

To find in which semicircle the ship is situated
Face the wind. If it shifts to the right you are in the right-hand semicircle, if it shifts to the left you are in the left-hand semicircle. If it remains steady but increases you are in the

direct path of the storm.

What to do (Figure 5.)

If in the path of the storm, run with the wind on the starboard quarter in the Northern Hemisphere and on the port quarter in the Southern Hemisphere at right angles to the assumed track.

If in the dangerous semicircle sail to windward away from and at right angles to the assumed track. If you cannot sail to windward, heave-to on the starboard tack in the Northern Hemisphere and on the port tack in the Southern Hemisphere.

If in the navigable semicircle, run with the wind on the starboard quarter in the Northern Hemisphere and on the port quarter in the Southern Hemisphere, away from and at right angles to the assumed track.

A normal depression may produce winds up to 100 knots, a cyclone 150 knots, and a water-spout may work up a blast of up to 300 knots. The latter, however, are of small diameter (200 to 300 yards) and short duration (a few minutes); getting caught by one of these is an Act of God and is not dealt with in this book—or in any other book that I have read.

If the reader proposes to cruise in hurricane areas he should—obviously—make a detailed study of the particular area before he enters it. HM Stationery Office, Atlantic House, Holborn Viaduct, London EC1 will, on request and for a modest price, supply him with literature covering the subject.

You should bear in mind that the instructions in the books are in general meant for ships more powerful than yours—ships that may be able to hold their course in conditions that may bring your boat down to bare poles. Therefore season those bits of advice about—heaving to on the port tack—running with the wind on the starboard quarter, etc. with a little intelligence and foresight.

5
Wind

Wind—by itself—is unlikely to damage a small boat fatally. If you are unlucky or careless enough to be caught by a squall of even hurricane force you may lose a few sails or, at worst, your mast, but apart from that a good little ship stripped and battened down is proof against wind-damage. It is, of course, theoretically possible for a tornado or a water-spout to generate winds sufficiently powerful to break solid wood, but I have never heard of this happening. In any case the discussion is barren; if you happen to meet that sort of wind there isn't a thing you can do about it except keep below deck and recite the Lord's Prayer sincerely and diligently.

The Beaufort Scale of Wind Force tabulates the wind from Force O (flat calm) to Force 12 (over 63 knots), the latter ranking as a hurricane. (See page 40.)

You are likely to over-estimate the wind velocity:

    (a) At night.
    (b) When the wind is against a strong current.
    (c) In heavy seas.
    (d) Sailing to windward.
    (e) When tired, wet, cold and hungry.

Under-estimation of wind velocity is a more rare fault, but can be dangerous at times. It occurs, usually:

    (a) When running before the wind.
    (b) When the wind is with the current.

Note: Owing to friction caused by waves the wind-velocity at sea-level is less than that recorded at nearby weather stations, whose anemometers are always high and unshielded.

Obstructions such as hills and mountains can cause some fearsome blasts; watch out for the *williwaw*—the squall that comes tearing down at an angle from steep mountain

slopes—the more you heel the harder it clobbers you. Also in the vicinity of land you may encounter the whirl-wind or wind-devil—a miniature waterspout spinning spume about like a furious ghost. Foil these by lowering or reducing sail.

A waterspout (contrary to popular opinion) is not a column of water. It is a miniature cyclone of such violence that spray and water vapour are torn bodily from the sea and whirled aloft. The area affected is small—200 to 300 yards—and they last but a minute or so. I have never heard of any ship being caught by one of these things, but I think they would wreak considerable damage. You are, however, unlikely to tangle with one in several lifetimes.

You can carry sail—reduced as necessary—in winds up to about 70 mph at which velocity ordinary canvas tends to blow out. Possibly Dacron or Terylene would hold, but so much power is now involved that even a tiny sail imposes enormous strains on everything, and if a sail takes charge in a 70 mph-plus gale you are in for a rare old time.

If you leap from an aeroplane without benefit of parachute you can console yourself—briefly—that no matter how far you fall you won't strike the ground at more than about 120 mph because at that speed the air resistance of your body neutralises the downward acceleration of gravity. It follows therefore that if you are standing on deck and a 120 mph gust comes along you are likely to be blown away bodily.

Much depends on circumstances, but in general one must accept that even under optimum conditions with a smooth sea one will be unable to work usefully or for long in winds in excess of 70 mph.

With wind speed in excess of that, the matter is taken out of your hands.

The moral is clear. Do the things that you ought to do and undo the things that you ought not to have done before conditions become dangerous or impossible. We shall come across this caution more than once in the following pages.

WAVES
(Approx. to Scale)

Figure 6

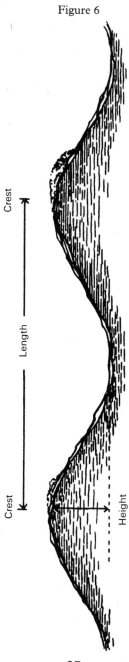

NOTE:
If forward slope exceeds 18°
a foaming crest forms.
If forward slope exceeds 90°
the wave 'breaks'.

Crest

Length

Crest

Height

'Period' is time in seconds between two successive
crests passing a given point

$$\text{Wave Speed} = \frac{\text{Length}}{\text{Period}}$$

6
Waves

The sea is the real enemy, persistently, ceaselessly seeking and finding every weak spot in your armour. Much of this warfare is silent—the slow rusting away of an iron nail that should have been copper, the quiet fatiguing of a faulty keel-bolt, the niggling little twists that unscrew the shackle pin that should have been locked. This kind of attack you can and must combat, chiefly by that five-minute-a-day check that counts for so much more than the big annual refit.

When angered by the wind the sea brings into action her shock troops—her waves and breakers. Against them careful maintenance by itself is insufficient. You must act, defend yourself, look ahead and, sometimes, counter-attack.

'I do love the sea!' How many times has one heard that statement? Dear old ladies strolling along the Esplanade, ulcered businessmen aboard the *Queen Mary*, office-bound wage-slaves Sunday-roaming through the docks, sun-tanned farmers from their dusty hinterlands—they all love the sea, simply and soulfully. But the professional seaman's regard for the element that supports him is a much more complicated emotion. He is bound to the sea by his calling. He makes his living from it, explores its surface and its depths, and—night and day—guards himself against its power. He is like a lion-tamer, controlling a strength greater than his, and knowing that constant precaution is his only protection. Yet the fascination of the sea enfolds him also.

38

When he must wrench himself into retirement he retreats into an environment that never compensates for the eternal challenge of the sea. The professional sailor reserves his affection for boats, and he never forgets that in the long run the sea gets all boats. Were he to be articulate about his feelings he would probably describe the sea as being a lovely, treacherous, faithless bitch.

Let us learn about the enemy. The wind blows over the ocean, and this causes waves. Nobody is sure how or why this happens, but there the waves are, and they are more complicated than you might think. The back-room boys have studied them in nature and in test-tanks. What they have learned is interesting rather than useful from the point of view of the small-boat man.

A few definitions, facts and theories: (Figure 6.)

Length of a wave. This is the distance between two successive crests. A Captain Mottez measured a length of 2,700 feet—which remains a record to date.

Period. The time that it takes for two successive crests to pass a given point. Length divided by period equals wave speed. Captain Mottez timed his wave at 23 seconds, but a Monsieur Bertin concludes that 2,950 feet length and 24 seconds period is a probable maximum. In practice wave speeds probably attain about 30 mph.

Height. Distance from trough to crest measured vertically. Maximum height appears to be anybody's guess, even amongst the experts. Mr Arago, for instance, feels that 26 feet is about the limit; the United States Air Force has a photograph of a hurricane wave which it estimates to be 100 feet high. The writer has seen waves on the Agulhas Bank that were certainly in excess of 40 feet; the general consensus of opinion averages out at about 50 feet maximum.

It must be emphasised, however, that these figures usually

Reprinted from *Brown's Nautical Almanac* by kind permission of the Proprietors, Messrs. Brown, Son and Ferguson, Ltd

BEAUFORT SCALE OF WIND FORCE

Beaufort Number	Mean Wind Speed in knots. Measured at a height of 33 ft. above sea level	Limits of Wind Speed in knots	Limits of Wind Speed in metres/sec.	Descriptive Terms	Sea Criterion	Probable Height of Waves in feet*	Probable Maximum Height of Waves in feet*
0	0	Less than 1	0–0·2	Calm	Sea like a mirror	—	—
1	2	1–3	0·3–1·5	Light air	Ripples with the appearance of scales are formed but without foam crests.	¼	¼
2	5	4–6	1·6–3·3	Light breeze	Small wavelets, still short but more pronounced; crests have a glassy appearance and do not break.	½	1
3	9	7–10	3·4–5·4	Gentle breeze	Large wavelets. Crests begin to break. Foam of glassy appearance. Perhaps scattered white horses.	2	3
4	13	11–16	5·5–7·9	Moderate breeze	Small waves, becoming longer; fairly frequent white horses.	3½	5
5	18	17–21	8·0–10·7	Fresh breeze	Moderate waves, taking a more pronounced long form; many white horses are formed. (Chance of some spray.)	6	8½
6	24	22–27	10·8–13·8	Strong breeze	Large waves begin to form; the white foam crests are more extensive everywhere. (Probably some spray.)	9½	13
7	30	28–33	13·9–17·1	Near gale	Sea heaps up and white foam from breaking waves begins to be blown in streaks along the direction of the wind.	13½	19
8	37	34–40	17·2–20·7	Gale	Moderately high waves of greater length; edges of crests begin to break into spindrift. The foam is blown in well-marked streaks along the direction of the wind.	18	25
9	44	41–47	20·8–24·4	Strong gale	High waves. Dense streaks of foam along the direction of the wind. Crests of waves begin to topple, tumble and roll over. Spray may affect visibility.	23	32
10	52	48–55	24·5–28·4	Storm	Very high waves with long overhanging crests. The resulting foam in great patches is blown in dense white streaks along the direction of the wind. On the whole the surface of the sea takes a white appearance. The tumbling of the sea becomes heavy and shocklike. Visibility affected.	29	41
11	60	56–63	28·5–32·6	Violent storm	Exceptionally high waves. (Small and medium-sized ships might be for a time lost to view behind the waves.) The sea is completely covered with long white patches of foam lying along the direction of the wind. Everywhere the edges of the wave crests are blown into froth. Visibility affected.	37	52
12	—	over 63	over 32·6	Hurricane	The air is filled with foam and spray. Sea completely white with driving spray; visibility very seriously affected.	45	—

NOTES—(1) It must be realised that it will be difficult at night to estimate wind force by the sea criterion.
(2) The lag effect between increase of wind and increase of sea should be borne in mind.
(3) Fetch, depth, swell, heavy rain and tide effects should be considered when estimating the wind force from the appearance of the sea.

* These columns are added as a guide to show roughly what may be expected in the open sea, remote from land. In enclosed waters, or when near land with an off-shore wind, wave heights will be smaller, and the waves steeper. The probable maximum wave height is reached by about one wave in ten.

refer to waves generated in a single and regular system of swells, and most observers agree that when a cross-sea exists (which is often) it is possible for these heights to be considerably exceeded.

Fetch. The uninterrupted stretch of water over which the wind can operate. As all seamen know, the longer the fetch the higher the waves.

It is the wave that moves, and not the water, the individual particles of which move in a circular orbit but otherwise stay put. If the wave slope exceeds 18° a foaming crest forms and blows down the forward slope of the wave. If the depth of water falls below about half the wave-length the wave trips-up on the bottom; the forward slope steepens, the height increases, and when the forward slope reaches 90° the whole crest falls down into the preceding trough—at which stage even a smallish wave packs a big wallop. Waves breasting a current are steeper and more closely packed than those running with the current; throw a stone in a river and see for yourself. You should remember this—it has great practical significance. Ordinary deep-sea waves are not likely to damage a properly handled and well found small boat. They may appear awesome, but the crest is loose water without much power in it. It is only when the wave slope steepens (due to shallow water, a boat running too fast before it, or interference by other waves) and the crest starts to tumble that the wave becomes dangerous. The occasional giant seas —the rogue waves—are the killers. I will deal with these in the following chapter.

Provided you do not resist it or upset it even a gale sea will not harm you. But thwart it and give it something to get a grip on and it will generate tremendous power. It can shift 30-ton boulders, curl up steel plates as if they were tin-foil, and generally toss things about and rip them to pieces. Add to this 'the explosive effect of thin pockets of air which may

7 Artist's impression of the wave that crippled the yacht *Coimbra* in the Atlantic.

be trapped and compressed as the crest curls over can cause serious structural damage if such a wave crest breaks and falls on to the deck of a ship'. (Kent)

To the novice it all sounds dicey to a degree. But—a fragile electric light bulb could ride out the worst typhoon undamaged. The small boat sailor knows that the reed that bends does not break; he believes in rolling with the punch, countering force with guile, that a soft answer turneth away wrath and that he who fights and runs away lives to fight another day.

7
The Ultimate Wave

There are other names for it—the occasional freak sea, the abnormal wave, the catastrophic sea. Even the staid Admiralty Pilot books refer gloomily to the existence of giant seas, although they steadfastly refuse to give any estimates of height, nor any counsel on what action should be taken on meeting the monster.

What we are to understand by this is a wave that differs from a normal wave in size and/or form in such a manner as to make it particularly dangerous to ships of all sizes. There can be no doubt that such waves do occur, although with any luck a man might spend a lifetime at sea without running into one. Their normal breeding place is the high latitudes and the tropical hurricane zones, and the blame for many a lost-without-trace tragedy can be laid on them.

Once only have I seen such a wave, and then I was—fortunately—not at sea, but standing on a rock on the beach at Cape Hangklip. There was a full gale blowing, and it had kicked up a tremendous sea which I was watching with some professional curiosity and wondering how a small boat would have fared in such weather. No skipper would have been carrying sail in such wind, of course; and any boat large or small would have been uncomfortable; but I judged that a good small boat properly handled would have ridden it out either running with warps trailing, lying beam-on (hulling), or riding to a sea-anchor. I was feeling comfortable about this—and then I saw the Ultimate Wave, and have never since

43

been casual when aboard a small boat in a big sea.

It rose far out, perceptibly higher than the surrounding seas, but what caught the eye was not so much the height but the shape, for the forward face of the wave appeared to be a vertical wall of water, and its general appearance was entirely at variance with ordinary gale seas.

Most people have seen how a big sea steepens on meeting shallow water, and how eventually (if the sea is big enough) the whole crest curls over and falls headlong down into the trough with a thunderous roar. Well—this sea looked like that, but with the horrid difference that it was falling continuously, so that it seemed like some white waterfall sweeping across the ocean at—maybe—30 knots or more. The speculation is inevitable—what happens to a small boat lying relatively stationary when it meets a vertical wall of water moving at 30 knots?

It is this subject I want to discuss, and we have to aid us the evidence of a number of people who claim that they know what happens from bitter experience—having learned the hard way.

Among these are the crews of such yachts as *Typhoon*, *Sandefjord*, *Les Quatre Vents*, all of whom believe that they encountered such a sea with results varying from the exciting to the disastrous.

The latest of these is Miles Smeeton, who tells of two such occurrences in his book *Once is Enough*. This is a book in grand contrast to many other yachting stories, written by lubbers who put to sea in cranky, parish-rigged abortions and get deservedly clobbered in weather that a competent boat and Master would take in their stride.

Briefly, the *Tzu Hang*, was a good little boat, 42ft loa, not particularly fast, but with sea-kindly lines. Her crew were Miles Smeeton, his wife, and young John Guzzwell. The yacht was well-found, sound, well-equipped and well-handled by seamen of the first water. She had safely ridden out many savage gales, and although at this time they were

bound east-about round the notorious Cape Horn they were reasonably confident of their own ability and of the qualities of their craft. Even when, nearing the Horn, they were caught in very heavy weather and forced to run under bare poles and towing warps, they were happy enough in the knowledge that their boat had carried them safely through weather as bad or worse.

And then, without warning, a great sea took the *Tzu Hang* and pitchpoled her stern-over-stem in a brutal somersault that left her a dismasted, water-logged wreck with her decks swept clear, doghouse gone, and indescribable chaos below. How they crept into a Chilean port under jury rig and re-masted and refitted their boat makes a brave and fascinating story.

But it does not end there. Once more they set course for the Horn—without John, who could no longer spare the time. Once again they hit the inevitable big depression. On this occasion they understandably were a little chary about running before, warps or no warps, and preferred to lie beam on, without any sail set—which is generally taken to be

8   The faked-in *Admiral Scheer* on the ultimate wave

a perfectly seamanlike habit. Once more the Big Sea got them—this time rolling the boat contemptuously over like a barrel, and again leaving her a barely floating derelict. How they made port again unaided finishes a story which I hope every cruising man will read.

From this and from the other accounts we can form a fairly clear picture of what happened in each case—and in every case the picture is similar. The moving wall of water rushes on the boat. Even before it reaches her, it picks up warps (if they are being towed) and carries them forward in loose bights to lessen or perhaps completely nullify their drag.

If she is riding stern-to she is swiftly brought into a stern-up, bows-down position. The bows dig in, and partly by the momentum of her heavy keel and partly by the onward rush of the sea itself she is thrown over to crash either on her deck, or perhaps, on her beam-ends should the heavy keel above take charge and wrench her over. Bow-on, the same thing must happen and, if lying beam-on, the boat is simply rolled over with the wave passing over it.

It would appear from accounts that if one has to make a choice in the matter it is preferable to be rolled rather than pitchpoled, but in either event you will be lucky to escape at all, and almost sure to suffer dismasting and fairly severe damage.

It is an upsetting thought in every way. It goes against the grain to believe that a condition can exist in which no amount of skill, courage, vigilance or equipment can save a small vessel from catastrophe. The majority of cruising men tend to avoid this conclusion, I think. They will affirm that the boat in question was running too fast, that she was pooped, or maybe broached broadside-to and was rolled by the following sea when off-balance—but few seem prepared to admit that a boat can be actually somersaulted.

In previous printings of this book I attributed figure 8 to the *Admiral Scheer*; this was also published in the first edition of *Once is Enough*, to show the kind of wave which

47

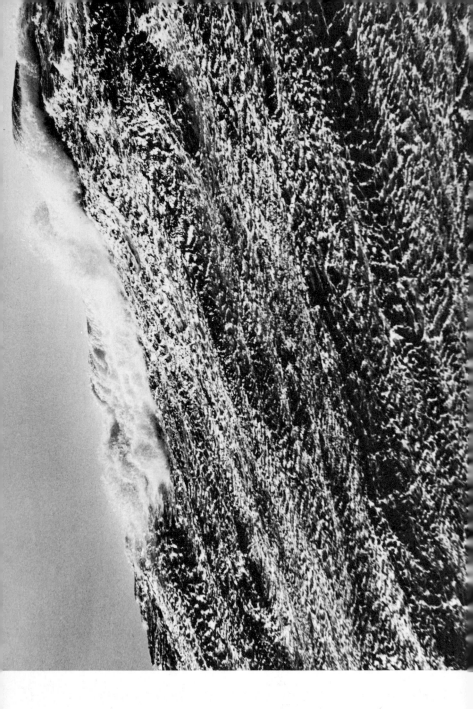

could cause a pitchpole. Smeeton has since revealed that the photograph was taken, without the faked-in battleship, off Cape Horn in the 1930's, but this does not lessen its impact.

I have discussed pitchpoling with a number of men with long experience of off-soundings cruising. All of them to whom I showed that photograph regarded it with horrified awe, and thereafter tended to regard it sidewise—and briefly. I have found general agreement that no ship on the Seven Seas could encounter a wave of that height and shape without at least being swept from stem to stern and suffering more or less severe damage.

As far as small boats are concerned, all felt that it was unlikely or downright impossible for any boat under 100ft loa minimum to rise to it and breast it. Most felt—as I do— that waves travelling at speed and with a forward slope in excess of 45° are simply not surmountable by any boat at all —and that includes the *Queens*. The vessel would rise to it as far as possible, but within seconds would either go through it or be smashed down—depending on size.

Faced with the phenomenon of a wave that cannot be surmounted, one casts about for some method of getting through it with the least possible damage. It seems that running with warps or hulling are not good ideas at all. What can be done?

How about oil? Supposing that oil would have much effect on waves of this shape—which seems doubtful—it would surely require a devil of a lot of oil. And the snag is that— because freak seas give no warning of their approach—you would have to spread large quantities of oil all the time on the off-chance that you will meet one. I suppose an oil tanker could afford that. A cruising yacht would never have that much oil available—although Smeeton suggests rather hesitantly that large built-in storm-oil tanks might help. Nobody knows, and on the whole, it does not seem to be a practicable solution.

The one device we have not yet dealt with is a sea-anchor.

9 Off Cape Agulhas

10 A wave breaking in shallow water

After considerable argument—sometimes heated—most of the deep-sea chaps seemed to feel that, although a sea-anchor was not the solution, the use of one might be described as making the best of a bad job. Even here there are nasty snags.

In the first place, let nobody suppose that a sea-anchor helps a boat to rise to a sea. On the contrary, depending from which end it is streamed, it does exactly the opposite, keeping the boat stem- or stern-heavy. But it would at least tend to pull the boat through the wave stem or stern first, which should end in less damage than somersaulting or rolling over—although one finds it difficult to believe you would have any masts left after the performance. Anyway, you stay right-side-up.

But—and a big but—what size sea-anchor is required to hold a small boat not only head (or stern) to sea, but also to counteract her buoyancy and the dynamic force of a great wave travelling at speed, so as to pull the boat right through the wave and out on the other side? And—when you have worked that one out—what are you going to make it of? Where are you going to stow it? What are you going to use as an anchor cable? And—and this is a good one—to what part of the boat do you propose to belay this cable?

I have had some experience with sea-anchors, and I suggest that you make the cable fast to some part of the boat that you can afford to lose. The problem is academic as far as most of us are concerned, but for some it may not remain so—because there are plenty of people (including myself) who propose to indulge in at least one more deep-sea, long-reaching cruise before we swallow the anchor.

I would like to widen the discussion group and get the benefit of some fresh ideas, so if you (yes—you who are reading this now) have any experience or knowledge of the cause of such seas, their shape and speed and—more important—how to avoid, circumvent, baffle, combat or endure them, pick up your pen and drop me a line. Between the lot of us we may be able to work out some solution or

safeguard. It would be good to think that some time in the future the Master of some little boat battling a heavy gale could regard the approach of the Ultimate Wave not helplessly, but with some degree of confidence.

8
The Boat

The right place to start guarding against heavy weather is on the drawing board before you start building your boat, and you will be faced from the start with the necessity to compromise all along the line. The ideal 'gale-proof' boat would be a sphere with no projections or indentations; in such a craft one could ride out the worst storm in safety if not in comfort, as witness the fact that the hollow glass floats used by Japanese fishermen to buoy their nets are often washed up undamaged on beaches half the world away from Japan. But it is difficult to see how one could sail or otherwise propel such a boat, or even exist happily aboard, so the shape of your ideal cruiser must depart considerably from this simple conception. However, we can get one clue from this— Nature prefers curves. (Don't we all?)

In general, then, the more curvaceous your boat the more sea-kindly she will be, and you should try to avoid flat surfaces as much as possible. But you have also to live and work aboard, and the hull must be shaped to lessen friction and resistance, so you must compromise again. It is a matter that has been studied since boats began, and by experience and trial and error types of hulls have evolved which appear to be the best compromise. The safest (if not the fastest) cruising hull is therefore round-bilge, with a generous beam and sweet lines—which is what the experienced naval architect usually arrives at if given a free hand and not bribed by a desire for speed or for economy in construction.

We may take it that the lines of a good conservative modern cruiser are the best we can do.

As regards material and scantlings we again have centuries of experience to guide us, and with honest workmanship and good materials you may rest assured that the hull will stay in one piece provided you don't hit something harder than water. On the question of superstructure, fittings, masting and rigging there is less agreement, and you can raise a good frothing argument any time you like by being dogmatic about these. There will be plenty who will disagree with much of what follows, and they are welcome to do so—provided that they bear in mind that the boat we are talking about is specifically built for cruising in places where really heavy seas may be encountered.

Superstructure. A flush deck is best. If that cannot be managed, then all structures should be kept as low as possible, made immensely strong, and rounded off to as close to a turtle-back as can be.

Port-holes. A number of small ports are better than a few large ones, and windows are to be avoided like the plague. If you must have a doghouse, go ahead and build it—but remember that if you get swept by a really big sea you stand a good chance of losing it.

Hatches should not only be strong, but capable of being battened, and all major entries into the hull should be constructed so that they can be closed by washboards or by some other closure able to withstand a hard clobbering. If you have a cockpit, it must be self-draining, with good big pipes. Avoid having lockers that open into the cockpit.

You should have at bow and at stern holdfasts—samson posts are best—of good size and as strong as they can possibly be made. A surprising number of cruisers have nothing to belay to on the stern deck except a couple of stupid little cleats which will pull out when the first real drag comes on them. Fairleads of ample size to take your biggest rope should be positioned to lead as nearly as possible in a fore-and-aft line—in addition to the normal mooring fairleads if the latter do not fulfil this function.

Rudder pintles and gudgeons should be as large and strong as possible, and most firmly fastened, and the same applies to your stemhead fittings, chainplates and other deck hardware. The guard-rail stanchions are an exception: they should be strong enough for their function, but not so deeply rooted into the structure of the boat as to inflict serious wounds if one or more are torn out by collision or other cause. Large ports should be fitted with deadlights. Windows are not a good idea, but if you have any then carry strong protecting covers that can be bolted over them—which also applies to skylights. Try to keep the deck as sleek as possible, without unnecessary protuberances and coamings. If you have a bowsprit it is nice to be able to house it in emergencies, but this is usually not easy to arrange on modern designs. Every underwater opening must have a skin-fitting of good size, well-fastened, and with a sea-cock—and keep the sea-cocks maintained.

Planked bulwark rails, if fitted, pose another little problem. We will assume that they are provided with freeing ports, but it takes even sizeable freeing ports a little while to drain off a full deckload of water—enough time, perhaps, for a second deckload to arrive aboard. The old Portuguese seamen had a dodge which is as good as any—they planked their rails with thin planking not very firmly fastened; a dangerous weight of water falling on the deck simply tore away one or more planks and automatically provided bigger freeing ports to suit the circumstances. Untidy, perhaps—but the principle is sound.

If you have a wind-ship pay no attention to any idiot who wants to streamline your hatches, cabin-top and other deck-proud prominences in a fore-and-aft direction—it is the one direction in which wind or water practically never streams over a sailing vessel. A moment's thought will show you that the only valid streamlining here is as near circular as possible.

Assuming fairly conventional layout, there is not much to be said about arrangements down below. See to it that everything that should be fastened is firmly fastened, and repress that urge for a large, unobstructed cabin—the further you fall the harder you hit, so there should be something solid to grab within arm's-reach of wherever you may be standing.

Rig

Sloop, cutter, ketch, yawl, schooner, brigantine, topsail schooner—all have their devotees. This is a matter for choice—plus remembering that 500 sq. ft. is as much as one man should be asked to handle in one sail.

Remember also that we are talking about a boat built specifically for hard weather—speed being a secondary consideration. This introduces one of the more difficult compromises we have to make, because for about 85 per cent of the time the ocean-cruising skipper is looking about for some place to set more sail to gain an additional half-knot or so. For about 10 per cent of the time the yacht will be tramping along blissfully with a wind 'designed' to suit her ordinary working sails, and for perhaps 5 per cent of the time the skipper is down to trysail or bare poles and wondering whether he would not have been wiser to take up date-farming in the Sahara Desert. What we want, therefore, is some rig that will carry a big area of working sail and which can be stripped easily and certainly down to bare poles.

The sail-plans should be kept inboard, and arranged to crowd the greatest possible sail area on the shortest possible masts. This brings to light the old controversy of gaff versus Bermudian, which has now been argued for so long and with such venom that protagonists stick blindly to their own choice and few are prepared to admit that the other rig has anything to recommend it at all. In addition there are a lot of yachtsmen who have never cruised under gaff, and a dwindling number who have never cruised under Bermudian.

Let us start the fight afresh and hammer a few sparks of common-sense out of the matter.

Gaff	*Bermudian*
Slower closehauled	Faster closehauled
More running rigging	Less running rigging
More windage	Less windage
Short mast— small fore-triangle	Long mast— big fore-triangle
Forbids permanent backstays	Permits permanent backstays
Forbids staying below the hounds	Permits staying below the hounds

It would seem that Bermudian wins the fight hands down. But wait—gaff comes up still punching:

Gaff	*Bermudian*
Faster off the wind	Slower off the wind
Gets more sail up there where the wind is	Cannot set topsails
Beam/mast-length ratio favourable for staying	Tapers off just where sail area wanted
Less chafe	Beam/mast-length ratio unfavourable for staying
Not sensitive to slack rigging	More chafe
	Rigging must be kept tuned
	Can jam irretrievably due to damaged track or luff-groove

Figure 11

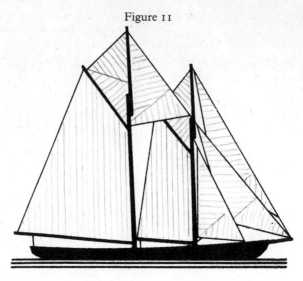

A Newfoundland Banks fishing
boat in her working clothes

A modern Bermudian yacht in her
working clothes

On my left, the winner—gaff!

A blow-by-blow analysis shows that gaff scores a resounding victory—bearing in mind that we are talking about far-cruising yachts expecting to meet heavy weather. The only points that Bermudian scores are racing points, and even here there is plenty of precedent for *modern* gaff beating Bermudian in top flight racing. But we are not going racing with a port close at hand and other yachts to assist us if we have a little trouble. We are going off into the blue, where if anything goes wrong we shall have to cope on our own, where safety and reliability means more than speed—and where by far the greater mileage will be off the wind. Under these circumstances gentlemen, Bermudian rig is a silly and unseamanlike abortion. Take a look at the two rigs in figure 11. The one makes use of all the available space, the other of about half the available space—and requires longer masts more sensitive to damage.

Consider a few possible emergencies and, make your choice:
You are under plain sail at night. A vicious squall strikes without warning, and you must get the main off her instanter —or else. Procedure with gaff: let the halliard go on the run (a modern wishbone gaffsail has only one halliard). We assume that you (as a good seaman) had taken up a little weight on the weather topping lift, so your boom is still under control. The gaff and half the sail may be dragging in the water to leeward, but you can sort that out at leisure. The selling point here is that you stripped her of the main instanter as required.

Now try doing that on a dark night in a 50 mph plus squall with a Bermudian sail. It'll be all hands to haul down on the luff with the helmsman trying to shake her enough to ease their task without flogging the stick out of her and the track-slides (or luff-rope) fighting them every inch of the way. If the mast whips under the pressure of wind and bends the track (or damages the luff-groove) well, the pubs are full of prematurely white-haired yachtsmen drowning the memory of the time that they got caught in a sudden squall with a jammed track.

Assume that the wind increases and that you have to get all sail off her and ride it out. The tall Bermudian mast now offers a lot more resistance, and whether you are anchored, riding to a sea-anchor, or drifting the ship will feel this. Every cruising man has noted how the Bermuda-rigged yachts lying at their club moorings are heeled sheerstrake under in a gale wind when their stubby-masted gaff-rigged sisters scarcely acknowledge the squalls. In addition the shorter gaff mast with its relatively wider base for staying is a much sounder engineering proposition.

Gaff-haters claim that in light airs and calms—'that damn gaff flogging about up there is a confounded nuisance'. One answer to that is that you can stop it from flogging by means of a vang and a preventer foreguy, but the real answer (for the cruising man) is that if the wind is that light he will be merely wearing out his gear and his nerves for little or no progress and he should lower the main and enjoy some peace and quiet.

Stop foaming at the mouth and regard figure 11. At the top, dressed in her working clothes, is a Newfoundland Banks schooner, a commercial fishing boat designed, built and rigged:

1 to keep the seas in any weather—because the Grand Banks produce some of the hardest conditions imaginable.
2 for weatherliness—the ability to claw off a lee shore.
3 for endurance to stay at sea for months.
4 for speed, because first boat home got best prices.
5 for ease of handling and economy.

All these conditions were functional; the Bankers were workboats, built to meet the demands of the sea and of their trade and, as often happens, Function begat Beauty. Look at that lovely, powerful schooner and admit that you have never seen a better-looking boat. Crew? 7 to 10—with cook.

Below the schooner is depicted her conversion to
Bermudian rig. This may be a bit faster close-hauled, but
running, reaching—or ocean cruising—the gaff version will
be the faster boat. There is no comparison—for our purpose
—between the two. The gaff-rigged boat, apart from
satisfying the eye, gladdens the heart of her skipper by
enabling him to hang up a whole variety of sails which
utilise every inch of the sparrage during that eighty five per
cent of light weather, and yet when stripped offers two
shorter, sturdier masts to the force of the wind.

There is a moral here. In general, commercial (working)
boats develop the optimum rig—a crowd of canvas easily
handled by a man and a boy, the object being to get the
boat from point A to point B speedily, efficiently, safely and
economically.

To get away from the nostalgic, we know that any yacht of
any size built and rigged in the modern racer-cruiser idiom
would in turn run rings round a Banker whether the former
were Bermudian or gaff.

In modern material and style the gaff will be a wishbone
gaff. Given a ketch, it can be controlled by a vang led to the
top of the mizzen and its gyrations in calm weather damped
or eliminated. Closehauled it can be trimmed in by the vang
to make the sail almost, if not quite, as close-winded as a
Bermudian sail.

For my money the ideal cruising rig is a ketch with wishbone gaff on the main and Bermudian (or maybe a Chinese
bat-wing sail) on the mizzen.

I have impeccable support for the wishbone gaff and for
reef-point reefing. Eric Tabarly has a sparkling record
proving that the wishbone not only cruises well but can
beat crack Bermudian racers boat for boat, and Bernard
Moitessier ($1\frac{1}{2}$ times round the world single-handed without
stopping anywhere) wouldn't be seen dead with roller-
reefing (or maybe that's the way he *would* be seen?).

9
Fatigue

Once upon a time—and this is a true story—there was a yachtsman making a single-handed passage in the Caribbean Sea. He struck a bad patch, about four days of heavy weather. When the wind moderated he was not at all certain of his position. So he took his sextant and tried to shoot the sun. He couldn't do this because:

    (a) he was unable to hold the sextant steadily.

    (b) he could see four? three? two? suns.

    (c) he could not do simple addition or subtraction.

So, having no option, he carried on sailing, and within a short while sighted a lone fisherman in a dinghy. He was delighted about this, because it meant that he must be near land, and he hailed the fisherman, asking his position. The fisherman made no response. He continued to fish without even glancing at the yacht. Evidently a surly type. So the yachtsman sailed on—and soon he sighted land and a small harbour. From this harbour a pleasure launch put out, crowded with trippers, and passed within 50 feet. He hailed the launch. Not a soul aboard answered or showed the slightest interest in his plight. Proper bunch of curmudgeons, he thought.

Anyway—he should worry. He had made landfall after a rough passage and had found a snug harbour. He sailed into the harbour and—because nobody paid the slightest attention to him (no Customs blokes, no medical officer)—he chose a clear area, got out the lead-line and found eight fathoms, and anchored. Then he dropped through the hatch, hit the cabin floor and flaked out for twelve hours. On awakening he clambered on deck. His yacht was securely anchored. But there was no harbour, no pleasure launches, no fishermen in dinghies, no land in sight. But—he was anchored in eight fathoms. He'd got that right anyway. The rest was pure hallucination—wishful thinking—brought on by sheer, overwhelming fatigue.

Fatigue is the small-boat sailor's greatest enemy, be he cruising yachtsman or commercial fisherman. Gales may come and gales may go, and a good little boat properly handled will ride them out, shake off the spray and continue on her way—because ocean cruising is statistically a good deal safer than riding round in a motor-car. Also cheaper, less ulcer-making, healthier and more pleasant. But it can at times be exhausting, and it is this exhaustion that leads to trouble. It fuzzes up the mind, dulls the wits. It becomes difficult to concentrate on the simplest problem—and the answer often comes out wrong. Making decisions becomes an agonising business; I have seen a chap sit for 20 minutes wrestling with the choice of opening a can of much-needed sardines or getting into his bunk for some much-needed sleep. In extreme cases—as noted above—exhaustion leads to dreamland illusions.

Fatigue is a spell cast over the human mind and body by three wicked Witches of the Lack Family. They work together, and their names are: Lack of Food, Lack of Comfort and Lack of Sleep.

Lack of Food is the least dangerous of these harridans. There is, usually, lots of food awaiting a can-opener. It may not be possible to warm the food—but if you are hungry enough and shovel it in, your stomach will accept it gratefully, and cope with it. The energy value is only fractionally increased by warming, and a healthy man can keep going for a long time without food.

This is not to say that I am against food. I've been eating

the stuff for years and it is my favourite dish, but, this is important, if you and/or your crew are tired, cold, wet, miserable and dispirited, a hot meal is a tremendous morale-booster. Five minutes after ingesting the grub everybody perks up, decides that the skipper's parents might have been married to each other and the impending mutiny is postponed.

Aboard commercial fishing boats that spend days and days at sea the cook ranks high in the hierarchy, and if you were to face the skipper of such a boat with the choice of sacking a good mate or sacking a good cook he would probably burst into tears and require the services of a psychiatrist.

The second witch is the beldam Lack of Comfort. You must try to circumvent this hag, because she can be dangerous. If your boat becomes a cold, dripping, damp, soggy hell, your bunk a clammy morass, and yourself shivering and soaked to the skin, you will not be able to function with much efficiency. This witch can be exorcised by going to great lengths to keep the interior of the boat dry by stopping deck-leaks and by muffling yourself up in layers of protective clothing while you are on watch.

You should try to ensure that you always have a change of dry clothing. In a smallish boat during a longish gale this is difficult to arrange; water is insidious stuff and it seeps up the trouser-legs and sleeves, down the neck and round the waist-band, so that after two or three wet watches everything you own is soaked. It is partly for that reason that the cruiser I propose to build is going to have a galley stove of the slow-combustion type—one of those elegant-looking affairs that burn continuously for months on end on a shovelful of coal or anthracite a day.

By arrangement with the cook, crew members may hang wet clothes on a drying rack in the galley. In dirty weather comfort is almost synonomous with warmth. When steering small yachts with cruising cockpits during very cold nights

I used to light the hurricane lamp, clasp it between my feet on the cockpit sole, and drape a blanket about myself from the armpits downwards. This keeps you good and warm from the waist down, but if there is rain or spray flying around and the blanket gets wet it creates a sort of a muggy Turkish bath atmosphere which penetrates all your clothing and makes you feel terrible when you discard the blanket. Also you are left with a wet blanket and at the moment I can't think of anything more repulsive than a wet blanket. This is not a recommended practice—it can burn holes in blankets, sea-boots and clothing, and it makes you socially unacceptable for a long time because you become permeated with a distinctive aroma of paraffin, scorched rubber, burnt cloth and honest sweat.

The real answer is to keep the boat dry below, to ensure that wet oilskins and clothing are not paraded through the cabins, to have good bunks with lots of blankets and to have several changes of warm clothing.

The worst of the witches and the one most to be guarded against is Lack of Sleep. Her spell does not operate when you are off-soundings, because no matter what the conditions, if you've got lots of sea-room and you feel sleepy you can put the yacht in a defensive position (hove-to, hulling, running or sea-anchored), curl up in your bunk and go bye-byes. If you are really tired you will sleep, no matter what sort of hell is breaking loose outside.

Sleep, Death's gentle Brother—
Sleep that knits the ravelled sleeve of Care
—is a precious commodity, and old Mother Nature insists that you indulge in it. You can take all the anti-sleep pills you like and resort to all sorts of stratagems and devices—but sooner or later you will fall asleep. Soldiers on guard duty (to avoid the unpleasantness of being court-martialled and shot at dawn) adopt a practice of resting their chins on their bayonets while standing at their posts. I have on a couple of occasions come across them standing thus, chin on bayonet,

eyes open—and fast asleep. As a commercial fishing skipper I have on occasion had my cabin washed out by a sea and, on coming off watch, thrown myself into a bunk that was a mass of squelching blankets, awash with sea-water (with a thick layer of drowned cockroaches)—and have slept like the dead.

For a singlehander this problem of sleep becomes serious when he is coastal cruising, or wending his way through islands—in brief, when vigilance is necessary 24 hours a day. It is also serious if you happen to be the skipper and/or navigator of a crewed boat because if nobody else aboard can navigate, you have no option but to instruct the helmsman to call you up at any change of conditions—if the strength or direction of the wind alters, if he sights a light, when certain landmarks, lights, beacons and so on come on to certain bearings. Which means, in effect, that you don't get much sleep. So, when cruising coast-wise, the navigator (who in small boats is usually the skipper) should not take a watch. He will be on call and will be called at all times of the day and night, and he must be allowed to hit the sack as opportunity permits.

As far as the rest of the crew are concerned, watches must be arranged to ensure that each man gets eight hours' sleeping time out of 24 hours. This is a minimum time off. The watch must be changed punctually; there is nothing more likely to cause bloody-mindedness than hanging on to a tiller on a dirty, wet, cold night for 15 minutes overtime because your replacement just doesn't feel like turning out on time.

Enforce this rule, because one of the effects of sleeplessness is irritability, and you can find yourself saddled with a snarl of personal feudings among your crew. A cup of coffee or, better, hot soup, is a great sustainer if it can be arranged, but the old tradition of knocking back quantities of rum to keep you going is strictly for the birds. Alcohol in any form gives you a quick, short uplift—followed by a quick let-down which leaves you in worse plight. The stuff has its virtues. It relaxes tension and relieves inhibitions but the time to take a snifter is not before or during a watch, but just before you tumble into your bunk. Skippers of successful commercial fishing boats do not allow any alcohol aboard. The American Navy follows suit, and operates on Cokes and ice-cream and the British Navy has now stopped issuing rum.

Getting back to the question of Lack of Sleep, Lack of Comfort and Lack of Food, I would say that the British Navy system is the best compromise. Come sundown the crew get together for a beer and a chat—and the bar is then closed until the next sun-down.

The single-hander with land close aboard faces a major problem in this business of getting enough sleep. There are a number of partial solutions. If there is some wind he can heave-to on a tack that will take him offshore, and grab a few hours of shut-eye—but if the wind changes while he is snoozing he might wake with a bump. If there is no wind he can let the boat drift—but here again he'll be in trouble if there is an in-setting current or if an on-shore breeze springs up. In certain circumstances he may be able to anchor for a while. Or he can trim his sails so that the boat is headed on a safe course and take a chance on the wind changing. The best answer to the single-hander's predicament is a reliable alarm clock. He should assess the situation, decide on one or other of the above courses and work out how long the boat will be safe taking into account possible changes in wind strength, wind direction and prevailing current. He then sets the alarm for that period, places it in some fairly inaccessible position and hits the hay. The idea of putting the clock in some hard-to-get-at place is because if you put it within arm's reach of your bunk when the blasted thing goes off it is fatally easy to reach out a hand and press the silencing button—all without waking up.

But if you stick the clock somewhere—like under the companionway, for instance—where you can't reach it, then you have to get out of your bunk to stop the infernal clamour and—being now awake to some extent—you stick your head through the hatchway and peer blearily around to size up the situation afresh. With a bit of luck you may find that you can reset the alarm and kip down for another hour or so. Sleep is a mysterious state. It has been closely, extensively and expensively investigated for many years by doctors, scientists, psychiatrists and other boffins who have written endless tomes and treatises on the subject. One interesting feature that emerged from these experiments is that even after prolonged wakefulness—up to the point where the subjects were in the hallucination stage—eight hours' sleep is enough to restore normality.

If you pick the bones out of this article you will find out that this matter of avoiding fatigue boils down to:

(a) eating regularly and sensibly.

(b) keeping yourself and your quarters dry and warm.

(c) getting about eight hour's sleep a day.

10

Shortening Sail

Reefing is a subject about which volumes have been written, but it will be treated briefly and sternly here. The whole history of sailing is a record of the adoption of methods of doing something more quickly, more easily or more efficiently. Blocks, double topsails, wire rope, anchor winches, Highfield levers—the list is almost endless, and no doubt every innovation was bitterly opposed by the fuddy-duddys of the era.

Today the scene has changed; mechanisation is all the vogue, and yachtsmen are inclined to accept any new gadget foisted upon them by the power of advertising and install it without intelligent consideration.

There is one criterion here that is all-important. Every sail you set must come down quickly and without argument when you want it down. The old square-rigger seamen knew about the importance of this, as witness their little verse:

> *Man that is born unto woman*
> *Hath but a short time to live.*
> *He goeth up like a foretopmast staysail*
> *And cometh down like a flying jib.*

If you have a bowsprit set your working jib flying— i.e. without hanking to a stay—and tack it to a traveller. When you start your halliard and outhaul it will blow itself down. You may prefer to hank your genoa and jib topsail, but bear in mind that you must hand them before conditions out in front make this a dangerous job. If all sails are inboard the hanking of working headsails is an acceptable practice, although I can think of pastimes more attractive than sitting on a reeling foredeck fiddling frozen-fingered with a lot of piston hanks. It's a matter of preference, but personally, bowsprit or no bowsprit, I would set all staysails flying and forget about hanks. With modern Terylene-and-wire halliards and a bit of muscle you can easily put more strain on the luff of the sail than there is on the stay, and because Terylene doesn't have much stretch you need to freshen the nip only occasionally. The only real advantage of hanks is that they help you to muzzle big sails by bringing them down in one place, but with a little clueful handling of sheet and halliard an unhanked headsail can be blown down on the deck more or less at your feet. In the kind of weather with which this book is concerned you will not be carrying any light sails, so we shall confine the discussion to working sails and storm sails.

As regards the reefing of headsails, my suggestion is that you don't. The average small sloop, for instance, should have three forestaysails—working, No. 2, and spitfire; if you have to reduce sail, strike whatever sail you are carrying and set the smaller sail. The principle applies to any other type of rig.

Reefing the Mainsail

Roller-reefing is a glaring example of the power of advertising to induce muddy thinking. It's mechanical, it's cute, it's clever, it's neat—and so yachtsmen the world over clasped it to their hairy bosoms, and probably the majority of yachts afloat are equipped with it in one form or another.

Take a dispassionate look at roller-reefing. Compared with conventional reefing it has two advantages—and only two. It requires less gear and it looks neater. Apart from these points it has nothing else to recommend it and a

Figure 12

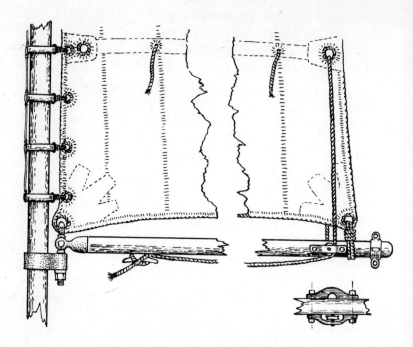

'Reef-tackle' Reefing

number of serious defects. (As I write this I can hear in imagination the roar of disagreement rising from yacht clubs throughout the world, from owners who have spent good money installing the gadget. Let's join battle.)

For the benefit of readers who may not know much about reef-point reefing Fig. 12 depicts a grand-daddy of the species. Sans mast-hoops and with modern flat-cheek blocks, and maybe a little winch instead of the cleat on the boom, it can be streamlined a lot, but the principle remains the same, and one can see why Moitessier wouldn't be without it because, as he wrote "—to reef the mizzen takes me one minute. The main, two." (His *Joshua* was a 36-ft ketch).

I had a big iron hook shackled at the gooseneck and when reefing simply hooked in the relevant luff-cringle. Theoreti-

cally, with a slack luff the cringle might slip off: in practice
it never did. I have also depicted a single deep reef only,
because any cruising man in worsening weather will keep her
going under working sail until she protests, and then put in
the deep reef without fiddling about with intermediate reefs.

To reef this sail, slack the halliard and hook in the tack
reef cringle; heave in and belay the fall of the clew reef
tackle—and you're reefed. The reef-points can be dealt with
at leisure. The boom will be cocked at a fair angle, but there's
no harm in that and if you don't like the look of it you can
adjust it by slacking the peak halliard. But the actual reef—
the required reduction of the sail area—goes in almost in
seconds, and provided your tackle is sound, it stays in.

Roller-reefing, apart from being slower, forms a weak
mechanical link at a vital point. Unless furnished with some
unhandy device it droops the boom into the cockpit. On a
dark windy night it is inclined to roll up other gear as well,
and it relies entirely on a ratchet and pawl or a worm and
pinion. If either of these slip or break you are in trouble—
you're not only suddenly unreefed, but you'll have to con-
coct some other way of reefing. In brief, it 'fails dangerous',
whereas conventional reefing fails safe.

When dousing sail your boom(s) must settle on to a
proper gallows or boom-crutch, and must be lashed or
otherwise locked in place without relying on the mainsheet
to keep it in place. A scissors-crutch is an abomination; it
will chop your fingers off one day—and serve you right for
having it aboard.

II

Storm Gear and Equipment

Any book on cruising will give you a list of what you should carry aboard in this line, but make sure that the following items are included.

Two anchors with ample chain and a warp—the latter preferably nylon. One anchor should be a heavy fisherman, the other a CQR or Danforth type. A third anchor should be carried as a spare.

Life-harnesses and lines. Various proprietary types are available with body harnesses, lengths of good rope and a snap-hook or hunch-hank at the other end to be clipped to a stay or some other support. One for every member of the crew, please.

One or more large-diameter hairy ropes 20 to 40 fathoms long according to the size of boat. For towing astern to create a drag when necessary; and for tying up and a dozen other uses.

Protective clothing, which should not be a long coat but jacket-and-trousers or overalls.

At least one lifebuoy of the type that lights up automatically as it hits the water. Keep it maintained.

At least one lifebuoy with a long line attached.

If you can get them, those little personal life-lights that clip to the shoulder. One for every member of the crew.

A reliable hand-worked bilge pump—something that can really shift water—and, if you have an engine, a mechanical bilge pump. See that the suction ends are get-at-able.

Oil—the more viscous the better. Old sump oil will do.

A sea-anchor. According to the books the maximum diameter should be 1/10 of the waterline length—but see Chapter 14.

The above, I repeat, is not a complete list—it is merely a reminder.

Cleats, ring-bolts and deck fittings generally must not be screw fastened; they must be bolted through to a backing plate under the deckhead. This applies also to winches, Highfield levers and similar fittings—except mast fittings, where you have no option but to screw them or attach them to a mast band. Fit some easily operated locking device to Highfield levers to prevent them being accidentally tripped. Lock the pins of all important shackles. Never permit the fall of any running rigging to be half-hitched. The only exception to this rule is the fall of a halliard being used to hoist and hold a man aloft.

Lanyards are better than rigging screws, which have been known to fail owing to unsuspected blow-holes or fatigue. But lanyards are a fearful nuisance—one is continually having to take the slack up and otherwise maintain them—so compromise by buying the best rigging screws on the market, specifying at least one size over-size, having them tested, fitting them, locking them and their shackle pins, maintaining them and hoping for the best.

In addition to the usual marline spikes, knives, spanners and pliers, always keep a handy-billy, a good, long, strong rope (nylon or Terylene if you can afford it) and a couple of sizeable, well-maintained snatch-blocks stowed ready for use. Also fit eye-bolts located so as to enable you, by hooking in snatch-blocks, to use your anchor winch to exert a pull in all conceivable places and directions without the rope fouling deck superstructures.

The use of nylon or Terylene rope for running rigging is a matter for the individual pocket. Their strength is fantastic—

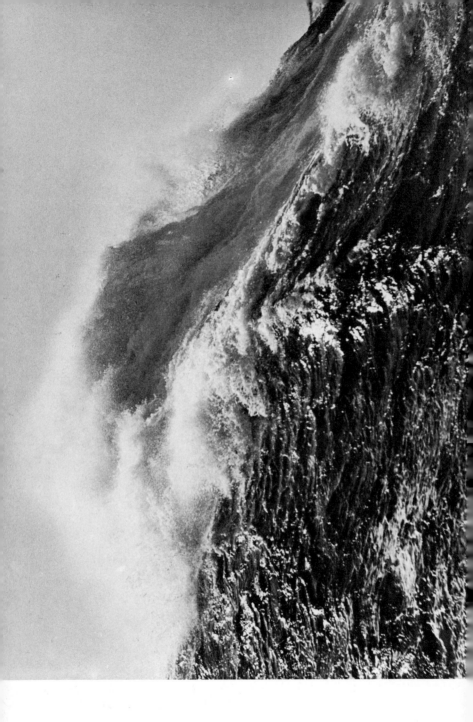

$\frac{3}{8}$ in. dia. nylon is said to have a breaking strain of about 3,700 lb.—but they cost a lot and are, of course, subject to chafe, although much more resistant to it than manila or hemp. Nylon, on account of its elasticity, is suitable for anchoring, sea-anchor warps, mooring springs, and the aforesaid long strong rope in the preceding paragraph, but not so good for halliards, where Terylene is better. A fair compromise for a yachtsman without unlimited means would be manila or hemp for sheets, Terylene plus wire rope for halliards, and a couple of coils of nylon for mooring and emergency use.

Much the same arguments apply to stainless steel wire for standing rigging—if you can afford it, well and good. But if you use it, make sure that you get the non-fatiguing wire; some kinds will still look as good as new after five or seven years but are liable to crystallisation in areas of vibration and can let you down with a nasty bump.

A couple of deck floodlights affixed to the main spreaders is an excellent idea—backed, of course, by at least two waterproof electric torches. While on the subject of lights, many cruising yachts mount their port and starboard navigation lights on side-boards lashed to the main shrouds. Avoid this: the side-boards are always fouling sheets and guys and in addition in a heavy blow when the wind strikes them at a critical angle they are likely to start a powerful and damaging oscillation. If your ship is rattled down do not use wood ratlines—for the same reason.

Immobilise the fore-and-aft gimbals of your steering compass—i.e. allow the compass to react to roll but not to pitch. Keep it thus in fair or foul weather.

12
Gale Warning

You're off-soundings, drifting without wind, the boat rolling and slatting in an unaccountable and increasing swell. The barometer is dropping steeply, the sky has a brassy glare, the air is humid, and you have that officially-recognised indefinable feeling that all is not well. It all adds up to the possibility (not a certainty) that you are in for a change of weather with the chance of a hard blow, and if you switch on your radio you may hear the weatherman saying that a depression is heading your way.

The first thing to do is to try to estimate what sort of a blow is coming—with the emphasis on the wind direction and probable changes thereof. If you are in a hurricane zone during the hurricane season check the indications and decide whether you are in the path of a hurricane. (See Chapter 4.) Don't go on a diet of fingernails estimating the probable or possible strength of the coming wind—there is nothing you can do about that, and worrying will only give you ulcers. Take all the facts you have at hand, season with knowledge, stir with intelligence, and draw a weather map on the chart. From this make the best guess you can of the nature of the coming disturbance, the wind pattern it contains, and its probable duration. Watch the behaviour of the barometer, and when the wind arrives and steadies, re-read *Tropical Revolving Storms* and get the probable bearing of the centre of the depression and the track. Your crew (if you have any) can busy themselves snugging the ship down, lashing and stowing, and getting the storm gear ready for use. All this shouldn't take long, and at this stage there is probably no need to shorten sail—you're a wind ship and you might as well use the wind while you can.

Get a good meal inside everybody, and take a stroll round the boat checking on everything. Anchors lashed? Deadlights and washboards ready for use? Stormsails, warps, sea-anchor, oil and torches all in order. Bilge pumps O.K.? All movables below stowed and lashed? Sump oil level correct and engine a starter? Life-jackets, life-lines and safety gear all present and correct—and crew knowing where they are and how to use them? You're all set—so sit down at that chart and consider your strategy.

Strategy

The first bit of strategy is to try to avoid tiring yourself. If you have a crew let them do most of the work—they may shortly need a skipper with a clear head not drugged by fatigue. The places to weather a heavy gale are, in order of merit:

> moored or anchored in a 'safe' port or haven;
> off-soundings in mid ocean;
> near land;
> anchored or moored in an unsafe port or haven;
> on a lee shore.

There's not much to choose between the last two as they're both very bad. Dealing with these in turn, there are fewer safe harbours than you might think, and more damage is suffered by yachts in port than on the high seas. A good berth alongside should be protected from waves and surge, and you should double or treble your warps. Remember also that the tidal range may be as much as 15 feet in excess of normal, and use all the fenders you can lay your hands on. Not many berths are safe—hence the battered hulks and embittered owners drifting forlornly around ports after a heavy gale. A

swing mooring is much better and usually safe, except against collision with runaway boats. You can and should insure against that.

In mid-ocean your strategy requires thought. If you have ascertained that you are in the path of a cyclone or cyclonic system you must make all haste, using engine if possible, to remove yourself from the track. See again the rules and procedures in Chapter 4, but when putting these into effect, however, you must bear in mind that they were written primarily for large ships that are able to maintain a desired course under conditions that will stop you. The chief thing to note here is that you must get the sail off her before conditions become unmanageable, after which you must fall back on tactics and procedures—of which more later. If you are in the vicinity of land you may be called upon to make some difficult decisions—and every one of these decisions must be made with the first basic rule of strategy firmly in the forefront of your mind. Never get caught in a gale on a lee shore.

It is vital to ensure that none of your plans involve any risk of this happening. If you are faced with what looks like being a long-lasting disturbance you must work out your strategy to cover contingencies perhaps days in advance. Let us consider situations that can arise in confined waters when faced with a gale.

1 *There is a good port or haven to weather of you*
If you would like to shelter there, get cracking with all speed. Even if you don't get there before the full force hits you you'll be getting into the lee of the land where the seas should be less and, incidentally, getting farther away from a lee shore, if any exists. Caution: is the wind likely to swing so as to make this weather port a lee port before you can get there? If you think it is, well, I told you that there were some tricky decisions involved in this section. You're the skipper, and it's up to you to decide whether to stay or move.

2 *There is good shelter to leeward*

Can you get there before the weather gets so bad that you cannot enter the port? Are you sure? Right—get going—fast! But bear in mind that the majority of leeward ports cannot be entered in heavy weather, and if you arrive to find that you can't enter—you've violated that first basic rule—you're on a lee shore and in trouble.

3 *A gale is brewing and there is land close a-lee with no good shelter*

Give her all the sail she'll carry, harden in your sheets, switch on the iron topsail, put her on the wind and grab sea-room. Don't take any chances on carrying anything away, but drive her up to the safety limit. Fly your racing flag if you like—just to remind yourself and the crew that you're competing in a race against an opponent with no scruples at all. Watch this matter of sea-room. It isn't something you can buy as required at the corner store, and most of the time you don't need it. But when you do it becomes a valuable commodity, and you may have to fight for it because there isn't any substitute.

The above are, of course, text-book cases, and in practice there will always be other factors that will affect your decisions. Your Pilot Book for the area will be a valuable, informative companion—though not always comforting; it should always be interpreted with the knowledge that generally it is advising skippers of boats more powerful than yours.

Tactics and Procedures

You've made that educated guess about the nature of the approaching depression, and you think it may be a full gale—the jumbo-size family packet. Your ship is snugged down and prepared for hard weather, your crew fed and briefed. After sufficient but nevertheless quick thinking, you've decided on your stategy, and the time has come to put your plan into action.

If your plan involves evasive action such as running for shelter or getting out of the path of the eye of a hurricane, or if you are buying sea-room, then you must keep her going as fast as possible with safety. Don't carry sail until handling or reefing becomes a dangerous job, but shorten in grudgingly only when necessary, and keep her at maximum speed; use your engine if you have one. She'll be a wet and lively ship and hard on the crew if and when you have to bend storm-sails, but your object is to get somewhere fast—so you have no option.

When you make port see that she is properly moored and protected and keep your crew aboard. They can take a run ashore to savour the delights of civilisation after the blow is over, but in the sort of weather we are anticipating it is almost certain that there will be one or more jobs for all hands—replacing warps, shifting fenders, if nothing worse. If you are anchoring in a lee, bay or bight, you can relax to the extent of setting an anchor watch whose main duties will be to check on chafe and dragging. Anchoring procedure is discussed in Chapter 15.

If you are passage-making well away from land and with no necessity to skeddadle out of the path of a hurricane centre then life becomes less complicated. There's no need to waste good wind, so keep sailing in a sedate manner suited to the increasing strength of the wind, reducing in good time to spare your crew, and omitting such niceties as intermediate reefs. If you are sure (or suspect) that the blow is going to be severe, a suggested procedure is: strike light sails in good time. Continue under plain sail until she starts protesting. Forget about reefing and storm-sails. Strip her bare and get down to survival-tactics while the going is easy. Let us assume that your suspicion about the nature of this particular gale is correct. You are, in fact, committed to coping with a wind in excess of 70 mph and gale-force seas.

13
Survival Tactics

There are several defence positions open to you. You can
heave-to, stream a sea-anchor from the bow, stream a sea-
anchor from the stern, run off before with or without
braking warps or drags, or, lie 'hulling', that is, strip the ship
and let her look after herself. Any of these can be combined
with the use of oil.

Heaving-to

The only sensible object in heaving-to is to prevent or lessen
the drift to leeward; your course will be roughly at right-
angles to the wind, and you may even fore-reach a little.
It is a tactic that should be adopted only if you have some
good reason for not wanting to go to leeward, because—
popular opinion to the contrary—heaving-to is a brutal
thing to do to a small boat and it can get you into a dangerous
fix if the wind increases.

In the first place your boat will lie at an angle of 6 points
or more off the wind and will have to bear the brunt of the
seas on a large and flattish cheek, she would obviously suffer
far less of a hammering if she could go over them lengthwise.
In the second place, even a tiny sail exposed under these
conditions imposes enormous strains on itself and everything
to which it is connected—sheets, cleats, stays, mast and, in
short, the entire boat. If anything parts you are in a whole
mess of trouble trying to sort out the shambles in conditions

84

not conducive to sorting out anything at all. Thirdly—and this is important—if the wind gets much over the 70 mph mark you will be faced with the unenviable task of striking whatever sail you have set and organising some other defence. If you make any mistakes you are likely to lose anything from a couple of fingers to one or more members of the crew, for the foredeck of a small boat now becomes a battleground with no holds barred and no quarter given. If you are caught on deck when a wave comes over green you will be irresistibly swept from whatever hand and foothold you have—and we must hope that your life-line is clipped to something strong. Until you have undergone this experience you can have no conception of the contemptuous ease with which a big sea will pluck a man clinging with the strength of desperation from his hold. So, as skipper, you must ask yourself whether you have the right to heave-to in worsening conditions if there is any prospect of your crew or yourself being asked to face that sort of hazard should the wind and sea increase suddenly. Fourthly—and this is not so important—a small boat hove-to in a gale is a detestable, lurching, slamming, deafening, streaming hell. All ordinary activities are out of the question; it is difficult enough to stay in your bunk, or even to think clearly. The moral is—don't heave-to unless you must.

Many owners of full-powered motor vessels advocate steaming into it. This is a matter of knowing what your boat can take, but it has never appealed to me for the simple reason that if anything happens to your engine(s) or if wind and sea increase to such an extent that you no longer have steerage-way you will, willy-nilly, be driven into a hulling position which may not suit your boat.

The other defensive positions are dealt with in later chapters.

14
Sea Anchors

This is a subject upon which everybody from skipper to cabin boy can lay down the law without much fear of informed contradiction—because although every yacht club has its quota of experts on sea-anchoring, any of them, if pinned down and tortured will eventually confess that his experience is limited to what he has heard about sea-anchors. Very occasionally one comes across someone who has actually used them—but how many times must you use a sea-anchor to become an authentic expert? I have used a sea-anchor three times and I have read every book about them that I have been able to beg, borrow or steal. Voss swore by them. Harry Pidgeon hadn't the slightest use for them. From the ranks of the deep-seamen you can collect evidence for and against and this writer believes that most of them are against, or at least dubious, about the matter.

On paper, of course, sea-anchors work like magic. (Figure 13.) The book says that the major diameter must be at least one-tenth of the waterline length and that the sea-anchor and all attachments must be made as strong as possible. The attachments consist of the sea-anchor cable, a tripping line, and a block with an endless line rove through it for hauling out oil bags. You make fast the inboard ends of the various ropes to something at the bow, chuck the whole caboodle in the sea—and there you are as per picture, riding happily head to wind and sea in a big smooth oil-slick that you can renew as required by hauling out another oil-bag to replace

Figure 13

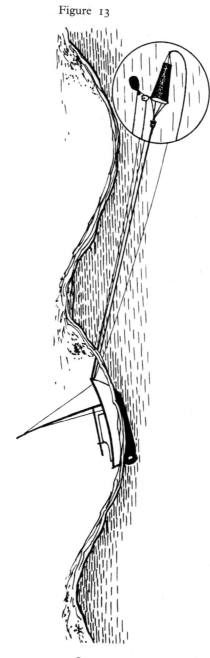

The 'Classical' Sea-anchor

87

an empty one. So where's your case against sea-anchors now?

The wave in the picture was drawn by myself, and it makes the picture a little less pretty. If the yacht is a thirty footer then the height of the wave shown is also 30 feet—which is almost a minimum height in the conditions we refer to throughout this book; we may well have waves of forty or more feet in height. Now—remembering that a sea-anchor exerts a tremendous drag—look at the picture and ask yourself whether the sea-anchor is going to help that boat to rise to the sea, even if by accident she happens to be heading into it. The answer, of course, is no; it is going to hold her bow down and tend to bury it and drag it through the sea, which is not a good thing.

As shown, there is nothing to prevent this classical sea-anchor from revolving—and revolve it will, winding all those ropes into one massive hawser; after which, if you took the mess ashore on dry land it would take you a couple of hours to disentangle your tripping line, let alone to use it. Assuming that we complicate the contraption further by adding an anti-rotating device such as a small anchor, it is unlikely even now that all four parts of line are going to remain apart in the smother, and they will be washed about each other and finish up again wrapped round the cable.

But let us take the most optimistic view and pretend that the four ropes stay obediently clear of each other. How do you fancy the job of sitting out on that foredeck and twiddling little bags of oil out to the sea-anchor in an 80 mph wind and plus-30 foot seas? I simply do not believe that this trick has ever been done in the history of small boats. There are several other methods of pouring oil on troubled waters, but when the sea gets bad enough to need oil you will not be able to sit about the foredeck hauling oil-bags in and out—in fact, lying to a sea-anchor head to sea as you are, you will probably not be able to use the foredeck with any safety at all.

There is yet another score against the sea-anchor which

does not show up in the pretty picture or in the manuals of seamanship. They all assume that the drag of the anchor will hold the boat steadily head to wind and sea all the time. In real life only a schooner or some other type of vessel having her windage aft of her CLR is likely to weather-cock and lie head to wind; you have only to watch yachts at moorings in a hard wind to realise that (whether fast to the bottom or to a sea-anchor) they sheer incessantly—and the more the wind and sea the bigger the angle of sheer. Which means that about 90 per cent of the time you will be meeting the seas bow-off to a greater or lesser extent, and the strain that this puts upon your anchor tackle is excessive. There is also a most unfair strain on the rudder.

Most yachts sheer less if the anchor is streamed by the stern. This is something that each skipper should test on his own boat. If she has a large open cockpit or little freeboard astern it is probably not a good idea.

The first time I tried a sea anchor was not of necessity but to find out how the boat would behave with one. The boat was a 52-foot fishing boat with a cruiser stern and a high bow with some flare. A wind of about 40 knots had been blowing for a long time, and the seas were about 15 feet high. We rigged the sea-anchor in classic fashion with tripping line, oil-bag tackle, and oil bag, and streamed it over the bow. When the strain came on it surprised all present by its violence, and it pulled the boat up almost as smartly as if she had been ground-anchored. The sea-anchor immediately rotated furiously, and in no time at all everything was wound up into a mess which took hours to untangle. The anchor performed its basic function well, slowing our drift to a mere crawl estimated at under 2 knots, but the boat sheered heavily up to 45 degrees both sides, and we were far more uncomfortable than we had been while either steaming or drifting.

The second time was with a 60-foot fishing boat in similar conditions but with a bigger sea and was for the same reason—purely experimental. This time we used a basic sea-anchor without any frills and furbelows, not even a tripping-line. Streamed by the bow we got about the same drift as above, and to get the anchor back we had to winch it in on a mechanical winch—the entire crew of nine couldn't budge it an inch by hand. Streamed by the stern, the boat lay much more quietly—as was to be expected because she had her windage forward—but she had a big flat transom which got slapped hard and frequently.

The third time was in dead earnest in a 25-foot yacht—a conventional 5-ton gaff cruiser with a transom. We were off Bashee Point on the East Coast of Africa, and in the Mozambique Current which was running at about four knots. The wind was plus-70 for certain, and might have been a lot more. It was also blowing directly against the current, which undercut the seas into most frightening steep-faced cliffs packed close together, i.e. the wave-length was abnormally short. It was night time, with plenty of lightning; I can only guess the height of the seas, but when we lay stern to on the forward slope of any wave there was at least a boat's-length of slope to spare ahead and astern. We were running before, stripped to the bare mast, and getting very wet indeed, as much under water as above it. We had plenty of sea-room—the nearest lee shore being, I suppose, the coast of Arabia about 5,000 miles distant—but even without sail we were travelling far too fast to suit my nerves, and the seas began to steepen ominously preparatory to pooping or broaching us. For this reason we decided to stream the sea-anchor to cut her speed.

There were three aboard, one being my wife, and with one at the tiller two of us had a rare old fight dragging the sea-anchor from the fo'csle through the cabin and on to the bridge deck, and then preventing it from blowing away. We managed to stream it at last, lying by the stern with cable and tripping-line only attached. It brought us up with a round turn, a sudden vicious drag that strained everything concerned to the limit, and the following sea seemed to pass right over the boat.

The trouble was that we hadn't thought out this bit of strategy intelligently—we had neglected the current. What we had done in effect was to drop the sea-anchor into a four-knot stream, and it was now doing its brutal best to tow us stern-first against wind and sea. We discovered later that our course over the ground even without the sea-anchor was actually taking us to weather. It was too much for the gear. About three waves later the big oak quarter cleat holding the cable tore away, and for a while we lay on the tripping-line, which incidentally provided a far more preferable drag than the cable had. Shortly afterwards the tripping-line parted, and the sea-anchor departed from us unregretted and un-mourned. We streamed a couple of hairy warps astern and came through safe and sound.

Now note this—it is important. The gale started in earnest at about 1600 hrs. when we were abreast of a distinctive shore-mark called Hole-in-the-Wall. From then on we were running before under the spitfire jib for about three hours, and under bare mast (and later trailing warps) for the remainder of the time—apart from the 5 minutes fun-and-games with the sea-anchor. Just on 24 hours later conditions eased enough for us to start making sail and closing the land —and our landfall was 20 miles to weather of Hole-in-the-Wall. In brief, while we were running with wind and sea a 4-knot current had pushed us against them at a ground speed of almost 1 knot. The reason is simple—water is 600 times denser than air.

To return to the virtues and vices of sea-anchors. They have many vices and only one virtue—they check drift. But that one virtue outweighs all the vices. The advice is the same as for heaving-to, never use a sea-anchor except when it is urgent that you check your drift. Always have a good sea-anchor aboard, and learn when and how to use it to the best advantage.

A Sail as a Sea Anchor

This idea was given to me by an old Italian who in his youth had been a fisherman in the Adriatic. The boats they used were open double-enders of about 20-feet loa and gaff-rigged. At times the Adriatic can produce a vicious short sea dangerous to any small open boat, and figure 14 indicates how the local fishermen dealt with the matter.

They unbent the mainsail from the mast but not from the boom or the gaff, and made a bridle with the mainsheet to each end of the boom. Mainsail, boom and gaff were then streamed over the bow on a short scope. According to my informant, the mainsail, lying flat on the water, caused the waves to vent their fury upon it and left a nice little slick in its lee in which the boat lay safely. When the sea dropped the whole lot was recovered, the main hoisted again, and off they went.

I pass the idea on for what it is worth, with the remark that it has all the earmarks of being well worth a trial.

Running Before and Towing Warps

This is a fashionable thing to do nowadays and the practice is based on sensible grounds. When running you are courting two dangers—pooping and/or broaching. The faster you run the more likely they become as the seas in your wake rise and steepen until they either come crashing aboard or pick you up bodily, slew you broadside on and tumble you over. Why the wake of even a small boat should have this apparently disproportionate effect on following seas has never been clear, but it does—and so you must keep your speed down.

The effect of towed warps is threefold. They act as brakes, they assist to keep the boat running straight, and they seem to have a quietening effect on the sea astern. There is very little technique about this. You take one or more big hairy

Figure 14

Sail used as sea anchor (see Chapter 14)

ropes and trail them astern. Increase the length, or the number until you have slowed down sufficiently to stop angering the following seas. (Figure 15.) In view of the apparent calming effect of trailing warps it would, on the face of it, seem to be better to tow a number of medium-length warps rather than one long warp, but I have yet to meet anybody who knows enough about this subject to be dogmatic about it—although I have met numbers of dog-matists who know nothing at all about it. But anyone who has seen how even a scattered barrier of floating or just submerged kelp magically tames a roaring breaking sea and transforms the sea around it to a harmless rounded swell must agree that the effect exists and that we might as well take advantage of it.

Make your warp(s) fast to something strong. They exert a lot more drag than you might expect, as you will discover when you start recovering them.

Hulling

This means that you strip your boat, lash everything firmly, and leave her to fight her own battles while you curl up below with a good book. This may seem a drastic abandon-ment of responsibilities, but it is good seamanship. The theory is that the boat will take up a position to suit herself (usually broadside on to the wind or nearly so) and her drift will create a slick to windward that will soothe the oncoming seas. You must, of course, lash your tiller as well, and you should know the best position for it by previous experiment. Use nylon rope or some other rope with a bit of give in it to cushion the rudder against shocks. It is an uncomfortable position, but it has its advocates, and as far as the records go it seems to be as safe as any of the other defences. It has additional merit in that it leaves the boat free of a lot of human beings badgering her to do something she probably doesn't want to do.

94

Figure 15

Scale: Length of yacht = height of waves

Running with the warps trailing

Study the accounts of small boats that have been damaged or come to grief in heavy weather at sea and you will find that in a surprising number of cases if the crew had simply gone to sleep and left the boat to her own devices she would have ridden the gale unharmed. Amongst the experienced cruising men who favour this idea are Harry Pidgeon (32-foot gaff yawl) and John Guzzwell (20-foot Bermudian sloop), and a goodly number of others.

15
Anchoring

If you can find shelter in a bay, a bight or the lee of land then anchoring might be not only feasible but advisable, but anchoring off a lee shore should be tried only as a final resort after all other resources have failed. It is assumed that you have the usual ground tackle which includes at least a fisherman type anchor and a lighter CQR or Danforth type.

On coming into your shelter pick what seems the best position (your Pilot Book may tell you this) in water as shallow as is reasonable having regard to surf present or possible and the possibility of offshore rocks and blinders and to the possibility of an abnormal tide. If you can find some solid object ashore to make fast to, do so by all means. If you are using a tree, pick a young and virile specimen, because in the kind of weather you expect less virile specimens may get blown down. One or more anchors out to seaward should hold you steady. If you can get another line ashore at about 45° to the first line it won't do any harm and may do some good. Bear in mind that if the coming wind swings through any considerable angle you may be in trouble with this type of moor, but I assume that you are not expecting this in this case. If you are faced with a cyclonic system then anchoring anywhere at all except in a recognised cyclone refuge is risky.

Anchoring (Figures 16 and 17) is another subject about which you can always raise an argument. The books say that you should anchor on a moor, i.e. with two anchors laid

Figure 16

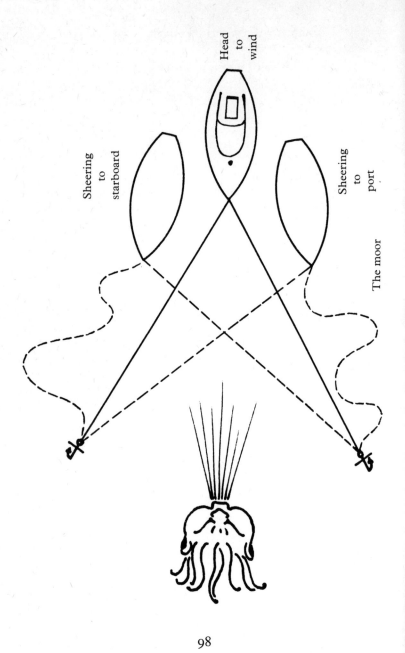

Head to wind

Sheering to starboard

Sheering to port

The moor

ahead and their cables forming an angle of about 45°. The theory is that this stops sheering. It may work with big ships, but yachts having their windage forward keep right on sheering, to bring full strain first on one anchor and then on the other; in effect you are lying to one anchor most of the time, and if the wind shifts . . .?

As every seaman knows, successful anchoring depends largely on avoiding strains on the anchor cable which tend to lift the shank of the anchor and lever the fluke out of the bottom. There are three main ways in which you can help here—by anchoring in shallow water, by giving a good scope of cable and by weighting the cable.

Figure 18 shows a method of anchoring in tandem in an emergency such as we are considering. You—obviously—use your heaviest chain at its longest scope. The end anchor should be the fisherman anchor on a hard bottom and the CQR on a soft bottom. Shackle the tandem anchor 3 to 6 fathoms back—more if you have a big boat and lots of scope —and drop them carefully, not in a rush, one on top of the other. The tandem anchor will not only give you additional holding power but will act as a weight to keep the shank of the end anchor parallel to the bottom. Additional weight can be added to the chain by sliding a ballast-pig down the chain attached to a bow shackle with a rope to regulate its position, but keep all weights towards the outboard end of the chain and not close up where they will tend to make the boat bow heavy. This rig is unlikely to drag on anything except the worst kind of bottom, but if you can do so lay out additional anchors. Every little helps.

Give all the scope of chain that you can, and see that the inboard end is made fast to something really solid; if you don't trust the bitts or the samson post, take an additional turn about the mast at deck level. Guard against chafe wherever the cables touch anything. Just aft of the bow fairleads make fast a length of springy rope, nylon preferably, to the cables and lead it right aft to your stern holdfasts,

Figure 17

Anchoring in tandem

End anchor

Tandem anchor

Sliding weight

Weight underfoot

sweating it in so that it takes the brunt of the snubbing. The bitter end of your anchor chain must be secured in the chain locker, not with a shackle, but with turns of good rope, so that if you have to slip and run you can do so with a sharp knife instead of tackling a rusty shackle with spanners and hacksaws. Get all sail off her—right off, unbent from the spars and stowed below. Bend on your trysail and spitfire ready to hoist, and see that they are lashed like an Egyptian mummy.

If you have the time and the means, drop a heavy weight underfoot to minimise sheer, not forgetting the probably abnormal tidal range, which means that this will have to be tended. Get your anchor light ready to hoist; it should be electric, because I have not come across any other kind that stays alight in 70 mph-plus draughts. Take some bearings and set an anchor watch to check for dragging and to guard against chafe. If you start to drag your anchors, there's not much you can do about it except to hope that they get a fresh grip or to slip and run for the open sea. Running your engine ahead will ease the strain somewhat.

It is mostly a matter of commonsense plus foresight. The boat in Figure 17, for instance, would be in a parlous situation if the wind were to swing through 90°, and the assumption is that her skipper knows that it won't. With the ship thus anchored and battened down you have done the best you can for her, and you must turn your attention to the crew. If the approaching disturbance bodes to be catastrophic, you must decide whether to get all ashore (if you can) and let the ship take her chance. Captaincy carries responsibilities.

16
Use of Oil

This is a chapter I would gladly hand over to some guest-author expert in the use of oil in heavy weather—one who had used oil lots of times and could speak from experience. But as I have never met such a person nor heard of one we shall have to be content with reading what the Seamanship Manuals have to say on the subject, what others have experienced, plus the writer's contribution from a small number of experiments.

Mechanisms for releasing oil are numerous. You can simply pour the stuff in the sea; you can hang oil-bags in such positions as seem good to you, or stream them out on drift-lines; you can dump it in the dunnegan and pump it out, or empty it into the bilge and pump it from there. Choice of methods depends on the particular circumstances and individual taste. The books give fairly explicit directions —under such and such circumstances you stream an oil-bag to windward from the weather bow, or discharge it over-board on the lee side, and so on. When going to the rescue of another craft in distress they all tell you to pump out quantities of oil to windward of the victim and wait until the slick forms round her. Beware of the books. Their methods might (or might not) work with big steamers, but every small-boat man I have met who has tried oil has hinted darkly that a good deal more empirical research into the subject is indicated. For instance, if you are going to the assistance of a small boat drifting in distress, by all means spread some oil to windward of her—but only a little for a start—and see what happens. We tried this once, and what happened was that it formed a lovely slick to windward of the patient, who never got near it; in fact, she drifted rapidly further and further away from it. After that we went to leeward and poured oil there, and in due course the other boat drifted into the slick and stayed in it for a short while before drifting out of it on the lee side. The moral seems to be that small boats drift faster than oil-slicks.

For the record, we tried a number of experiments from a fishing boat and from a sailing yacht in fairly rough seas but in what might be called optimum conditions because we were not in any danger and could go about the business calmly and quietly. For what they are worth, here are the results:

Oil-bag on sea-anchor. This was was the time the sea-anchor revolved and snarled things up. A nice slick formed to weather of the sea-anchor.

Hulling and spreading oil from the weather and the lee side. A nice slick formed well to weather of the boat.

Running with trailing warps and spreading oil from the bow. A nice slick formed well astern.

Hove-to. A nice slick formed well off the weather bow.

To cut a long story short, our oil never failed to form a slick—somewhere where it was useless. The only time we ever got into the middle of a slick and enjoyed its protection was when we steamed to weather with the fishing boat and parked her in the middle of one, keeping her there by occasional use of the engines.

The effect of even a small quantity of oil on a rough sea is extraordinary. A half-gallon of SAE 50 spread over hundreds of square yards of water must be reduced to a film that can only be measured in thousandths of an inch. But that iridescent layer smooths out great tumbling crests as they meet it, robbing them of all their fury. There must be plenty of horse-power involved in those crests, and what happens to it is a mystery to me; it seems incredible that it can all be absorbed without trace in a micro-film of oil.

The conclusion reached by all involved in these tests was that what is wanted is some device that will continually release oil from a position constantly maintained at half to one mile to leeward of the boat involved. Some sort of float, perhaps, with a metal sail? Or a kite towing a floating container? Not a satisfactory chapter, and letters from readers who have anything to contribute in the way of experiences or ideas on the subject will be welcome. One thing that every skipper who has used oil is certain about—it smears your boat with a filthy, slippery, treacherous film that takes a lot of removing later on.

17
Power Boats

In general the skipper of a power-driven vessel in hurricane conditions should adopt the same precautions and procedures as set out for a sailing vessel. For both types of craft the idea is to stay afloat—in one piece. This can be concisely condensed as follows:

1 If you make more water than you can pump out you will—sooner or later—sink.
2 If your boat comes to pieces through wave action or being driven on a lee shore you will have to swim.

There—in 37 words—you have the gist of this book. It is an accepted practice for powered boats to heave-to in heavy seas by steaming into them at just sufficient speed to maintain steerage-way. This is uncomfortable, but it works up to a point. That point is reached when the speed required to maintain steerage-way cannot be maintained or, more likely, involves crashing onslaughts and poundings into a head sea which are likely to start one or more planks or otherwise damage the hull structure or the superstructure. When matters reach this stage you have no alternative but to stop your engine and treat your boat as an unpowered vessel. Nevertheless the power vessel has advantages denied to the sailing boat. She can steam directly into the wind and (a point much overlooked) the slipstream from the propeller over the rudder gives her much more direction control at low speed.

As skipper of commercial (power) fishing boats operating

off a coast notorious for frequent and savage gales I tried out all the standard practices. Steaming into it, hulling (lying broadside-to), sea-anchors, oil-bags, and running before (with or without towing warps). As far as I am concerned, running before is the safest and most comfortable defence. You roll with the punch and, with a small boat this robs the following seas of much of their sting. Apart from the question of comfort this is important from another point of view: most powerboats have boxy deckhouses with windows, and a smashing sea can wreak a lot of damage on these superstructures. Check the design of your exhaust-pipe. When the engine is running the gas-pressure will usually prevent water from reaching the engine, but if there is any possibility of flooding when the engine is idling or stopped you should fit a sea-cock or make some other arrangement.

The captains of some of the 40-knot Crash-boats have been quoted as saying that when running before they could maintain speed without being broached or pooped by getting on the forward slope of some individual wave and staying there by adjusting their speed. Never having owned a 40-knotter I wouldn't know: it sounds fairly dicey, but maybe it works. But I have on several occasions heard the skippers of comparatively low-speed craft (under 20 knots) advocate the practice of out-running the seas by going before them at full speed. This is pure clap-trap. In the first place a gale sea will be travelling at maybe 30 knots—so the ordinary power vessel can't outrun it. In the second place if the skipper tries to outrun the seas at anything less than the speed of the seas themselves he is courting disaster. The only speed for running before is the slowest compatible with maintaining steerage way, and if the design and windage of your boat is such that she can be kept on course by 'sailing' under the pressure of wind on her superstructures (and perhaps towing warps as well) it is better not to use the engine at all.

Many small powercraft have large non-self-draining cockpits. A heavyweight canvas or Terylene cover most firmly secured will keep a lot of water out and save you the labour of pumping continuously, and you should have such a cover. But even the strongest Terylene cover is likely to split at the seams and/or tear out its fastenings under the impact of a heavy sea coming aboard. The sad fact is that non-self-draining cockpits are simply not a good thing for small cruising boats.

Bear in mind that in really heavy weather your engine is more likely to give trouble than in ordinary conditions. One major cause of this is the surging of the fuel in the tanks which stirs up sediment and condensed water lying in the bottom of the tank. Most owners appear to have a sublime faith in the ability of the fuel filters to cope with dirty fuel. This confidence is not shared by myself—or, for that matter, by the people who make fuel filters, who will be the first to expatiate on the merits of keeping your tanks clean. The answer? Keep your tanks clean. Drain out water and sediment and periodically open them up and clean them out. When topping-up see that the fuel passes through a filter *before* it reaches the tank. And if you have large tanks they should have baffle-plates to prevent surging. A second cause is the surging of the oil in the sump. Good marine engines are designed to eliminate malfunctioning due to this, but if your boat has an amateur-converted car engine you are likely to have trouble on this account. Another matter is the varying strain imposed in the engine by the propeller as the latter races or digs-in. The only thing you can do here is to tend your throttle to minimise these strains and to generally baby the engine.

If you have to move fast, to get out of the track of a hurricane, for instance, there is another matter to be considered. It does not seem to be generally realised (even by powerboat owners) that a marine engine and a car engine deliver power in different fashion. A car travelling even at speed along a level road will have its engine revving fast, but to maintain a steady speed the hp required is only that sufficient to overcome friction of moving parts and wind resistance. A propeller, however, puts an engine under load continuously; a marine engine therefore must do the work of the engine of a car which is climbing an endless hill in top gear. For this reason manufacturers of marine engines talk of maximum hp rating and continuous hp rating and recommend that the latter be not exceeded except in emergencies. Many commercial marine engines are governed so that it is not possible for the driver to exceed the continuous rpm rating. The point to be noted here is if you continuously run your boat engine at maximum rpm its useful life can be measured in hours.

Racing of the propeller if and when it is lifted into loose water or clear of the surface by excessive pitching of the boat is something for which (as far as small craft are concerned) no really effective counter has been invented. About all you can do is to try to anticipate when racing will occur and throttle back just before it happens. It is a wearisome and not always successful occupation, and to the mechanically minded the sound of the engine practically groaning as it takes up the sudden strain of the submerging propeller is distressing.

Decanting of fuel from drums into tanks, or of oil into sumps must be an operation that can be carried out in any weather, and you should have suitable hoses, funnels, etc. to enable you to do this. If you carry any large container for spare fuel (such as a 44-gallon drum) it must be lashed as solid as a rock. A length of rope round its middle will not do: the rope will stretch and chafe and you will have the exciting and dangerous task of chasing round after about a quarter of a ton gone mad. Wire or chain strops with rigging screws for tensioning are best, and fasten them to something that won't break or pull out.

18
Open Boats

The history of the sea abounds with sagas of small open boats which have made ocean passages of thousands of miles and have survived heavy gales. A well-designed open boat, properly equipped and handled, has a good chance of weathering even a savage storm. There are, however, a lot of ifs and buts in this chapter.

In the first place it cannot be too strongly stressed that proper design of the boat is as important as skilled handling. A well designed boat may even save a bad crew, though the best of crews may not be able to save a bad boat. Sail or power, inboard or outboard, ensure that before you put to sea you have aboard the following, at the minimum, equipment:

Lifejacket for each crew member.

Anchor and line.

Spare rope—120 ft.

Lifebuoy—or a couple of inflated inner-tubes, one of them tied to a spare line.

Distress flares. They cost little and may save your life.

Electric torch—preferably the waterproof type. The international distress signal is · · · − − − · · · (SOS) repeated at short intervals.

Bucket, of a type with a good strong handle. For bailing and for use as a sea anchor.

Another receptacle for bailing, in addition to the bucket,

and not of jam-jar proportions. There is no small-boat pump that can shift water at anything like the rate of an apprehensive bloke wielding a four gallon can. See that it has a comfortable handle and that the edges don't cut into your hands. (The can will weigh 40 pounds when full of water.)

Positive buoyancy. If the boat does not have built-in buoyancy tanks attach two, or more, four-gallon containers as high in the boat as possible, and lash them firmly in place.

Oars and rowlocks.

Steering crutch on the transom to enable you to unship your rudder or outboard and ship an oar as a steering sweep. This will give you more positive directional control. The rudder functions only when the boat is moving through the water—but a steering sweep acts as a lever.

Square all loose gear, including bailers, rowlocks, floor-boards, so that it can't wash out if you are swamped. Do not let fine, calm sunny days tempt you to shove off without the above equipment. Old Mother Nature is unpredictable; within half an hour, or less, she can change her mind and land you slap in the middle of a raging wind-storm.

Every day of every year some hundreds of thousands of people put out to sea and inland water in little open boats. Every year some thousands of them are drowned. Now mark you this: if those casualties had carried the equipment and had followed the precepts laid down in this Chapter, the majority would have survived.

If you do get caught out make every effort to get as close to safety as possible by rowing, sailing or motoring, but get into a defensive posture before the sea makes any of these pastimes dangerous. The only defensive posture for a small open boat is to keep her head-to-wind. You will not be able to do this by rowing or sailing, and you cannot rely on an engine, inboard or outboard, to keep going under such potentially treacherous circumstances.

If you have a mast and if you can unstep it in the conditions (which is not very likely), do so. Then lie to a sea-anchor if you have one. If you have no sea-anchor collect all the loose gear—mast, boom, floorboards, etc.—with the exception of your flotation gear and bailer, lash them together with a rope and use them as a sea-anchor. If it is a sailing dinghy you might try using the sail as depicted in figure 15. The drill is to use every device and every effort to keep her bows-on to the seas and to get the water out of her as fast as it comes in. Concentrate all weights (including the crew) towards the centre of the boat or a little aft of that—experiment to see which she likes best. If she tends to sheer try, by using an oar as a steering sweep through the stern crutch, to ensure that she meets each crest head-on. If you have a second sail you may (doubtfully) be able to stretch it over the boat as a foredeck to shed at least some water. Every little helps. There is not much else you can do now except to try to attract attention, and to tie a spare length of rope around your waist.

If you are swamped or capsized stay with the boat and don't attempt to swim to safety unless you are 200 per cent certain that you can make it. Two hundred per cent—that's right—because in these circumstances safety is always at least twice as distant as it looks. If you can, lash yourself to the boat. There will be lulls in the seas, and during such times try to right the boat and free her of water—you've not got much else to do, so why loaf? Most of the time, however, your main problem will be the effort of merely hanging on—which is why I mentioned that length of rope around the waist. If the boat has turned turtle there is a subsidiary problem as to what you are going to make the rope fast to. I can't help you here; it depends on the individual layout of your boat, and you must try to make some plan. If you are drifting shorewards and have to beach through heavy surf the advice is the same—stay with the boat as long as you can. The temptation to surf in on your life-jacket may be almost irresistible, but if the breakers are heavy it is better to leave this as a last resort.

If your boat is right-side-up you may try to bring her in through the surf. Do not try to surf in bows-first on a crest; in the kind of sea envisaged you will almost certainly broach-to and be rolled. Keep her bow-on to the breakers—and still with your sea-anchor streamed. Before the crest of each wave strikes row hard into it or steam into it if your engine is still going (which is most unlikely). If the boat broaches or capsizes in surf, get away from her and from your sea-anchor lash-up because in the turmoil of a tumbling crest you could get a nasty crack from either of them.

There will always be times when men in small open boats find themselves in heavy seas through no fault of their own, but the moral of this chapter is really this; if you voluntarily put to sea in a small open boat in the face of threatening weather or a gale warning and find yourself in a whole mess of trouble you will at least have the consolation of knowing that you are getting what you asked for. You might also, before shoving off, reflect on the fact that if you get into trouble you may also be endangering the boats and the lives of the people who deem it their unpaid duty to come out and rescue you.

19
The Crew

To say it again—captaincy carries responsibilities, and (assuming that you are the skipper) the members of the crew are your chief responsibility. Crews come in all shapes, sizes, ages and sexes. They may be paid hands, amateurs, or paying guests, but almost without exception you will find that (after the first hard blow) they accept implicitly that their duty is to the boat and her skipper. Your task is to see to it, tactfully but firmly, that they know the ropes. It is also your duty to safeguard them.

For a delivery trip, i.e. a business affair of taking a boat from point A to point B for profit in as short a time as possible, a paid professional crew is best. Both you and they will be short on the romance of the sea, anxious to complete the voyage and to return to the flesh-pots, and in addition you have a financial hold on them. For this kind of voyage the amateur crew is not recommended; you are liable to get a bunch of out of work, pleasure-bent beachcombers whose main idea is to hang around every port for as long as the local people are prepared to stand them drinks for the privilege of listening to 'gales I have weathered' stories. For the long cruise the paying crew is usually the best. You get—to be blunt about it—a better class of person; people who, no matter how they have inherited or made their money, have felt the call of the sea strongly enough to sacrifice the social round for the inevitable discomforts of a small boat long-voyaging. They will be ham-handed at first, but eager to learn and capable of learning.

Whether you are singlehanded or with crew you must try to keep yourself fit and fresh in the face of an emergency. Ideally, the skipper should never stand a watch; he should be on call twenty-four hours of the day. In the event this is not always possible, but do try to pass on to the crew all the routine jobs, and spare yourself. Too many amateur skippers give way to a (compensatory?) urge to beat their breasts and go around screaming obscenities under the impression that this will show how tough and salty they are. This is a mistake, probably engendered by seeing too many films. In real life good skippers, amateur or professional, are almost invariably quiet-spoken men who couple a knowledge of their job with the ability to live amicably with their fellow men. Both qualities are needed; Captain Bligh of the *Bounty*, for instance, was a first-class seaman but a bad skipper; James Cook and Admiral Anson, on the other hand were not only skilled mariners but also generous and humane—and more successful.

This is not to say that the crew are to be allowed to do as they like. If one of them makes a mistake, you must immediately point it out to him and get him to do the job properly, showing him how if necessary. From time to time, human nature being what it is, you will come across some character who is a pathological troublemaker. Bawling him out won't help, and upsets the rest of the crew. Get rid of him at the first opportunity.

Food and clothing are of paramount importance. A man with a full belly and a warm skin will stand up to hardship and fear as long as need be; hungry and chilled, he will crack sooner or later—usually sooner. If you reach the stage where everybody is sitting around like a lot of sick fowls awaiting the crack of doom—feed them. You'll be surprised to see the way they'll perk up. Dishing out tots of rum (or any other alcohol) to put strength into the crew is another fallacy. The effect is temporary and brief, and the last stage is worse than the first. Save the bottle to celebrate the end of the gale. Comfort is important. How you berth your crew will naturally depend on the layout of the accommodation, but give them the best you can in the way of a bunk and a good mattress. Also—because every human being occasionally feels the need for privacy—try to provide a nook for each crew-member, even if this amounts to no more than sliding curtains that can close in each bunk.

The height of a gale is no time to start teaching the crew how to batten down, stream a warp or, in fact, for teaching anything at all. Before you leave your first port the crew should know:

1 where everything is
2 what its function is
3 how to use it.

As far as possible, share your knowledge and decisions with the crew. In short, keep them in the picture. I stress the fact that all this advice applies to the ocean-cruisers. The skipper of a racing yacht may—in fact, must—hammer both boat and crew without mercy if he wants to win. On a far-reaching cruise the pattern is different. There is no frantic hurry; you will all be living in confined quarters for a considerable period, and, as skipper, your job is to ensure that your yacht completes the voyage without mishap and, preferably, arrives at her destination with all aboard still on speaking terms.

20
Survival after Disaster

This chapter is strictly outside the scope of this book, in which I have gone to a good deal of trouble to explain how not to court disaster. However, supposing you do find yourself adrift, the following information and hints will (at best) increase your chance of survival—or (at least) give you a bit more time to meditate on the fact that the whole unfortunate business would probably never have happened if you'd read this book properly and listened to what I've been telling you all along. You can be adrift in a variety of ways—all more or less embarrassing—which we deal with hereunder.

Adrift without a Boat. For purposes of this heading the term boat includes raft (rubber or other), i.e. you are in the drink with or without a life-jacket (but I'll allow a bit of driftwood if you can lay your hands on it). The score here is to keep calm—which is a lot less easy than it sounds. I found myself in this predicament once, and I can tell you that panic wells up like a bubbling flood. If you give way to it you'll drown within the next few minutes—and that's all there is to it.

Keeping afloat is obviously the next matter. Oilskins and seaboots should be discarded immediately, but—contrary to old waves' tales—ordinary clothing does not drag you down. On the contrary, the air enmeshed in it provides some positive buoyancy (for a while, anyway) and in addition some insulation against the cold water. If you can strip off jacket, shirt or trousers and tie knots in the arms or legs you may, by waving them around, entrap air in them and thus contrive do-it-yourself water-wings.

A life-jacket automatically keeps the head above water. Without one, you can, of course, tread water—but this is exhausting, and it is better to try to float motionlessly. Fat chaps have an advantage here; most of them float on their backs with a bit of freeboard, but many thinnish people find that when they float not much more than the top of the head shows above water and the mouth and nose are immersed. There is nevertheless still a future for such minimum-buoyancy types—without having to tread water or even able to swim.

There are two methods of continuing to breathe—without physical exertion. One is the jack-knife drill, which requires that the body be doubled-up at the hips, with the arms stretched above the head. You will then float bottom-uppermost—and it doesn't matter how much or how little of the said bottom sticks out of the water. When you're getting to the end of a lungful of air, bubble it out under-water, and straighten the body to surface for a fresh lung-full. I've tried this (in the swimming pool) and it works, and I once saw a film of toddlers who couldn't swim a stroke making a sort of game of it. So it's worth bearing in mind. Or you can lie on your face and, when you need air, turn the head sideways and gulp a breath—as in the crawl swimming stroke. If there's a sea running it will make matters much more difficult.

Your viability depends to a large extent on water temperature. If the water is very cold you must hope to be rescued quickly. (I mention this merely as a matter of medical interest—there's nothing you can do about it.) If there are several of you in the water, get together. If possible, tie yourselves together. The total buoyancy will be the same, but it'll be spread more evenly and the ups-and-downs evened out a bit. Also a group is easier for rescuers to spot than a single person.

There remains the question: What to do about sharks? I spent some time considering this problem with the most intense concentration, because on the occasion when I had to swim for it I was in waters notorious for man-eating sharks. A large number of experts have advanced their theories as to the best way of scaring off sharks, and we are pretty safe in saying that there are about as many theories on how to scare sharks as there are experts on the subject. (One also has an uneasy feeling that there is much the same difference of opinion amongst sharks.) During this swim of mine my first reaction (*viv-à-vis* the matter of possible sharks) was an intense regret that I wasn't surrounded by a whole crowd of other people in the same dicy plight. This was a most reprehensibly selfish thought—but the fact remains that even a largish shark is unlikely to eat more than one bloke, so the more blokes there are the better the individual chance of remaining uneaten.

The most usually recommended scare systems are: splashing like mad to frighten the sharks; knocking two stones together; shouting underwater; swimming underwater straight towards the shark and climbing on the shark's back and sticking your fingers in its eyes. To deal with these in turn:

Splashing. I don't agree with this. Big fish when wounded, and shoals of small fish when frightened, splash vigorously—and it is likely that this is one of the signals which attract sharks to a potential meal.

Knocking two stones together. This is probably a good gimmick—it is an unnatural noise and might tend to make a shark more cautious. But, you'll be a man of most exceptional foresight (and equally exceptional personal buoyancy) if you find yourself accidentally in the drink clutching two stones which you have thoughtfully provided as shark-scarers. It's a nice thought—but an unlikely occurrence, so we can perhaps forget about it.

Shouting under water. This also has the earmarks of being a good idea. Try it by all means.

Swimming underwater towards the shark. I would not be surprised if this wasn't about the best defence. I used to catch sharks commercially (for bait) and know something about them. They have very little reasoning power—but bright and almost unerring instinct. The sight of a largish animal of absolutely extraordinary shape swimming directly towards it might well ring some kind of a danger or caution alarm in a shark's tiny brain.

Sticking fingers in sharks' eyes. Why not? Can't do any harm—and might possibly do good. I'm sure that even a shark doesn't like people trying to gouge its eyes out and whaddya got to lose (except your life)? Give it a bash, anyway—and write and tell me how you got on.

If we have dealt with this matter somewhat flippantly it is simply that we might as well put the brightest side of what is essentially an unhappy subject. A man (or men) adrift in the sea with no rescue in sight or expected can rely on nothing but phenomenal luck for survival. Nevertheless, there is yet one more rule to be stated and observed—never despair because Lady Luck visits more often than one might expect —or, maybe, she favours her persistent suitors. There have been hundreds of cases (especially in wartime) of men being rescued after four or five *days* in the water. There have been other instances of men who have fallen overboard, unnoticed, from steamers in mid ocean—and have been sighted absolutely by chance and rescued by another steamer hours later (in one case almost 24 hours later). And so the final admonition here is—stick around as long as you can.

(Nobody has enquired what happened on that occasion

when I fell into the drink. It isn't really germane to the issue, but in case anybody is interested, there was land in sight, I wasn't eaten by sharks, and I crawled ashore after a long swim. But I was absolutely exhausted—had it not been for the fact that the water was warm and that I was wearing a life-jacket I do not think I would have made it.)

Adrift in a Boat (*Dinghy or Raft*)
This section is conveniently divided into two time-eras—B.C. (Before Catastrophe) and A.D. (After Dunking).

Before Catastrophe. Any skipper embarking upon a deep-sea voyage should rehearse in imagination and in practice some sort of boat drill. This will obviously depend on the equipment available; your vessel may be large enough to boast a lifeboat and a dinghy, and all but the tiniest boat can (and should) stow an inflatable raft.

This book is not a treatise of life-saving equipment. It is written for seamen—and if your emergency equipment is not adequate and well-maintained and your crew not trained to handle it then you are no seaman.

Attention is drawn to one or two matters which are often overlooked even aboard otherwise well-managed yachts. Firstly, remember that catastrophe can strike in fair weather as well as foul, and the life-jackets should not be stowed in some un-get-at-able place and broken out only in rough weather. Secondly, in addition to the fresh water in your built-in tank(s) you should carry a supply in portable containers—jerricans or plastic bottles. This is not only a commonsense provision against your tank springing a leak, but has obvious advantages if you have to abandon ship. Also keep, in a small canvas bag a knife, a hand compass and a fishing line and hooks. These are minimum requirements—you can elaborate on them almost *ad lib.* according to the size of your boat and the state of your pocket and/or nerves.

As soon as you know or fear that disaster is imminent, a

priority is to try to make your plight and position known. A radioed Mayday call is an obvious method, but with or without radio if you think there is any chance of visual signals being seen use rockets, flares, and all the other distress signals in the book. Of equal urgency, of course, is to get your practised (I hope) boat drill into action.

Derelict. Before dealing with Abandoning Ship we must consider the cases in which whatever misfortune has befallen has immobilised the boat without destroying it— probably the loss of masts and/or engine power, leaving the hull afloat and (more or less) intact. You are, in fact, derelict. If one has to make a distinction, this is the least of the two evils, because there is almost always a good chance of rigging some sort of jury rig (even on a power boat) that will enable you to make way through the water. Much will depend on the amount of damage and of spoilation of food and fresh water, but basically your task is to get the boat moving and to head for land.

You may have to make a tricky decision here—and this paragraph applies whether you are derelict or have abandoned ship (see below). Whatever jury rig you may contrive is likely to be a poor performer both as regards speed and windward ability. The inclination will be to shape course for the nearest land. But if that land is to weather of you or up-current of you some objective calculations must be made (and without any wishful thinking) as to whether it would not be better to square away and make for a leeward (or down-current) destination—even though it is further away. It could easily happen that instead of *trying* to close land 100 miles to weather it would pay you to make for a haven 1,000 miles to leeward.

Abandoning ship. If your boat is sinking you must abandon her before it is too late and take to your lifeboat (dinghy, liferaft or what have you).

The catastrophe may happen suddenly—leaving you little time to provision, apart from what is already in the lifeboat. Or you may have a chance to salvage and stow gear and equipment. In either case it is important to know what to grab first—and as you read further you may be surprised to note that Food has a comparatively low priority. The object is to ensure (as far as possible) that you will be able to sustain life in an open boat (or on a raft) for what may turn out to be a long time. The requirements for sustaining life are (more or less in order of importance):

1 Air: five minutes deprivation kills—but it is free and in abundant supply.

2 Maintenance of body temperature: extreme cold can bring about death by exposure quickly, sometimes within minutes. Prolonged high temperature can cause heat-stroke and/or dehydration, but this is a more delayed process.

3 Water: without water your life-span is one to five days, depending on conditions.

4 Sleep: the priority of this is difficult to assess. It is here placed above food, because lack of sleep will finish you off more quickly than lack of food. On the other hand the need and desire for sleep will triumph over the most appalling discomforts—and in any case sleep is not something you can store in a canvas bag for emergency use, so this priority is much of an academic question. We can fairly safely assume that you can and will sleep.

5 Food: how long you can survive without food depends on a variety of circumstances—amongst others, ambient temperature, body condition, expenditure of energy. But lack of food takes much longer to kill than lack of air, water, warmth or sleep; no medical man would so much as raise an eyebrow on hearing that some castaway had survived for twenty or even thirty days without eating.

Armed with the above knowledge, come the cry 'Abandon Ship' you at least know what to grab first. You will (we hope) not be naked, and you may prefer to take the chance that the clothes you are wearing will suffice to keep you warm, but if you have any time at all muffle yourself in the thickest garments you can find in a hurry, and grab a couple of blankets. That leaves water as top priority. Stow as much as you can—and this will be where those jerricans or plastic bottles will come in handy. Now you can start raiding the pantry—but in a selective manner. The various official Seamanship Manuals of different countries have different recommendations—but as you will not be shopping in a supermarket your choice will be limited. The criterion is to go for the compact, high-energy foods that do not require a lot of water for digesting. Fats, sugars, condensed milk, biscuits, sweets, raisins, dried meats—that sort of stuff. Forget about canned beans, vegetables, fruits and most varieties of canned fish—they usually have a high liquid content and are, weight for weight, less energy-packed than solid foods. I have never tried it (and hope I never have to try it), but I reckon I could live for a long, long time as a castaway on a straight diet of water, condensed milk (sweetened) and honey—and, of course, fingernails. Obviously don't take anything that will putrefy.

Distress Signals. Everything is important in this packing list and distress signals are no exception. Time and again one reads of steamers passing within sight but not seeing, and one can imagine few things more disheartening than not having any means to attract their attention. So include flares, rockets, smoke canisters, all the distress signals you have, and electric torches.

Navigational Equipment. Some kind of a compass is pretty well a must. As mentioned earlier, there should be one with the boat. Charts, sextant, Almanac, Tables and a watch— if you have time.

First Aid kit, naturally. And every time you have a moment to spare, chuck in more warm clothing—especially blankets. Blankets are most useful; apart from keeping you warm, they can be made into awnings to keep you from heat-stroke, used as sponges to sop up rain, rigged as sails— even used as nets to catch fish.

At this stage you can afford to pick and choose a bit—if you haven't already safe-loaded your lifecraft. There is one item to which I would give very high priority—a sheet of heavy duty plastic material, and the bigger the better. I would, in fact, have a whacking great sheet stowed permanently in the lifeboat. It has endless uses: a shelter against spray and wind; a boat-cover to shed waves; a rainwater-catcher *par excellence* and a fish net. In addition it can function as a crude still when suspended from the corners over a bucket of salt water so as to form a shallow basin; the heat of the sun causes water to condense in droplets on the underside of the sheet and trickle to the lowest point to drip into a suitably placed receptacle.

Command. It is quite essential that someone must be in command of this Operation Survival right from the start. For the purposes of this chapter it is assumed that this unenviable task is your responsibility.

If there are a number of survivors one of your most excruciating moments may come immediately, arising from the stark reality that a small boat or raft has a limited carrying capacity. The manuals deal with possible consequences of this in an unemotional way by stating that when a boat is filled to capacity no attempt should be made to pick up other survivors, but this evades mention of the possibility (even probability) of other survivors making desperate and determined efforts to scramble aboard. They will have to be beaten off. As Master you will have two agonising decisions: firstly to decide when the boat is loaded; secondly to enforce the order to rap drowning people over the knuckles.

Rationing. On paper, the daily ration of food and water is easy enough to work out—it is the supply you have aboard divided by your educated guess as to the number of days you are likely to be adrift. In practice this calculation is complicated by other factors. In the first case, the daily ration must be sufficient to sustain life, and the *minimum* here is about two-thirds of a pint of water and six ounces of concentrated (high-energy) food—sugars and/or fats. But your crew will be neither happy, healthy nor active on this diet. The British Admiralty recommends that a daily issue of $1\frac{1}{2}$ pints of water and about 1,700 calories of food be maintained until supplies are exhausted; it translates this into $3\frac{1}{2}$ ounces each of boiled sweets, toffee, sweetened condensed milk and biscuits. The ration must be issued with absolute impartiality. If anybody is very ill (from some other cause than lack of food or water) you will have to assess whether he is dying and, if so, whether his daily ration should be continued.

You may be able to supplement your supplies by catching rainwater, fish or birds. Rain should be collected by spreading out sails, tarpaulins, oilskins, etc. as catchments and by using any absorbent materials (even down to handkerchiefs) as sponges. One method suggested by the British Admiralty is to cut or bend a tin or some other stiff material into a chute to fit round the chin and jaws to catch the 'run-off' from the head. Rainwater should be issued before the 'stored' water, because it is liable to spoil sooner.

Whether or not to drink seawater is a vexed question. The Admiralty books state that the crew are to be prevented —by force if necessary—from this practice, and there is no doubt that imbibing much of the stuff will lead to delirium and death. But there is a school of thought that maintains that 'small' quantities of seawater may be mixed with the fresh water with advantage. The tricky question here is 'What constitutes a small quantity?' You will have difficulty in getting any medical man to give an opinion on this, and I think most of them would set their faces against drinking any seawater at all.

The moisture-content of fish is comparatively salt-free—but unfortunately fish (and birds) require a lot of water for digestion, and should not be eaten unless the water ration is sufficient for this.

Hurricane Warning

1 Abnormal behaviour of the barometer.
2 A big unaccountable swell.
3 A brassy appearance of the sky.
4 An indefinable feeling of uneasiness.
5 High cirrus cloud radiating from the centre of the disturbance.
6 Unusual panicky behaviour of sea-birds.
7 Radio Weather Reports.
8 Sudden puffs of wind—hot and cold.
9 A thickening and lowering of clouds towards the centre of the disturbance, accompanied by a rapid increase in wind velocity and—perhaps—lightning on or over the horizon.

Check List

1 A substantial meal for yourself and crew.
2 Batten down all hatches.
3 Check electric torches.
4 See that your storm-sails are ready for hoisting.
5 Make sure that your engine is a starter and 'a goer'.
6 See that your anchors and all movable gear on deck are securely lashed.
7 Make ready the sea-anchor and/or towing warps.
8 Secure all movables below deck.
9 Test the bilge pump(s).
10 See that life-lines, life-jackets and safety-gear are present

127

and correct—and that the crew know where they are and how to use them.

(Read Chapter 12 of this book)

The right spirit. Almost as important as the food and water ration is a bountiful supply of optimism. Men can and do become sick with despair—both mentally and physically and thus hasten the end. Buoy up the crew with accounts of the many, many castaways who have survived weeks and months in open boats. Tell them of the two lifeboats of the *Trevessa* sailing over 1,500 miles to safety. Remind them of the Chinese steward who drifted on a rubber dinghy around the Indian Ocean, living literally off the sea on birds, fish, barnacles and seaweed scraped from the bottom of his boat, and dew and rainwater soaked up in little bundles of kapok salved from a life-jacket—*for thirteen months;* and who, when finally rescued, was still healthy enough in body *and in mind* to stand up in his bobbing cockleshell and bow politely to his rescuers.

The four basics. To sum it up, the essentials for survival are but four—and they apply with equal force to a king in his palace as to a castaway upon a raft. They are: water, shelter, food—and Faith. Let us set no priorities here—you need them all to be saved.

Postscript

I leave you with a boat with few gadgets or chromium plated innovations—in fact, a boat that seems in many ways old-fashioned. But the sea is also old-fashioned. She will not be a fast boat, but she will be a good-looking boat because beauty and function go hand in hand. Throughout this book the emphasis has been on catastrophic conditions—hurricanes, gales, giant seas and other abnormalities. The novice might gain the impression that this business of ocean cruising is a risky undertaking. Let me remove that impression. Given a good boat and using ordinary common-sense precaution, you are, statistically, more likely to come to an untimely end when crossing the street than while ocean cruising.

The vast majority of your sailing hours will be free of anxiety or care. There will always be something to occupy your time—navigation, maintaining the boat, inventing a new recipe, or lying on the deck at night watching the stars while the ship steers herself. No telephone, no telegrams, no salesmen or importunate visitors. But occasionally the Lord will send you a sample of hard weather to keep you up to the mark, to teach you to appreciate the halcyon days and to remind you that the only currencies the sea honours are duty, vigilance, skill and endurance.

Index

131